MW00960835

ITALY
Over 300 Critical Tips You Need to Know Before You Go

Other books by the Author:

ITALY The Best Places to See by Rail, An Alternative to the Escorted Tour

ITALY Skip the Hotel and Stay at a Palace for the Same Price Live Like Royalty

BOB KAUFMAN

**The Gelato Press
916 Pleasant Street
Norwood, MA 02062 USA**

ITALY   Over 300 Critical Tips You Need to Know
Before You Go

Copyright 2020 by Bob Kaufman and The Gelato Press
of Norwood, Massachusetts, USA

All rights reserved.   Printed in the United States of
America.   Absolutely no part of this book may be
reproduced , distributed or transmitted in any form or
by any means, including photocopying, recording or
other electronic method without the prior written
permission of the publisher, except in the case of brief
quotations embodied in critical reviews and certain
other non-commercial uses permitted by copyright
law.

Information included in this book is believed to be
correct at time of publication.   However, the reader
should be cautioned to verify all routes and rates
stated by the author with known websites on the
internet.   Train times stated and travel times are
approximate.   Hotel   and   attraction   rates   are
approximate.   Please consult their websites for current
information.   The bank exchange rate of the Euro vs.
the US dollar used in this book is approximately $1.12
to purchase one Euro.

Cover photo of Italian pizza and glasses of white wine in Chianti, famous vineyard landscape in Italy (Tuscany) by Tomas Marek.

Back cover photos: Lise Beane and an outrageous gelato; The Gladiator's of the Coliseum with Lenore Brownstein and the Author; and Lenore Brownstein in the La Mincana Winery and Vineyards near Padova (thank you Artenio Dal Martello).

The author can be reached at
thegelatopress@gmail.com
-or-
Bob Kaufman
The Gelato Press
916 Pleasant St #9
Norwood, MA, 02062 USA

ISBN-13: 9781677189281

Acknowledgements:

Lenore Brownstein my life partner, for being sequestered with me for three months (especially for those comments about the Italian driver's) while I wrote this book and, thank you so much for your other inputs, assistance in editing and comments; Suzzette Freedlander of the DSPOT for her cover design and book layout; Michelle Delacourt for her expertise in MS Word; Lise Beane, Jane Hall-Curran and Dr. Hermano Queiroz, for their recent photos and/or reviews; on the back cover.

MEET THE AUTHOR

Bob Kaufman has a passion for travel in Italy and Spain. He wrote his first book in 1983 about telecommunications. Although discontinued, it's still available on Amazon. He thought he would write his third book on Italy and share over 300 tips he learned while operating tours of Italy. Bob has lots of experience on this subject. He ran those expensive group only tours. He is the past President of National Travel Vacations, Inc. (NTV) and for over 30 years specialized in group only tours on contract to travel agents in the USA.

Bob's an Eagle Scout, and when he is not digging clams in the summer on Cape Cod, he is enjoying the beautiful American Southwest in the winter with his travelling companion and partner Lenore. Bob and Lenore love Italian food and of course gelato.

TABLE OF CONTENTS

INTRODUCTION

In September of 2019 I made my 31st trip to Italy. Yes, you read correctly thirty-one trips! Wow. All of my trips have been different. With the exception of my group tours in the past which were always Rome, Florence and Venice, we decided to stay at a 1,000 year old castle in Limatola and visit Alberobello, the home of the cone shaped Trulli houses.

Over the years I have helped numerous people plan a vacation (Europeans say holidays) to Italy. Many of them have been first timers and many asked me what they could do on their second or third trips. I was always willing to suggest an itinerary. What is more important is that I was willing to share hundreds of critical tips with them that most of the time they would not find in a travel guide or even on the internet.

After years and years of sharing these "critical tips" I decided to compile them in a book and share them with all those folks who want to visit Italy and enjoy it the way we do.

I call these tips "critical". A good tip in Italy would be to enjoy the regional wines. My favorite is Frascati from the region about 20 miles southwest of Rome. That's just some good advice; certainly most would not call it a critical tip.

However, a critical tip is "We, for some reason wound up in a ZTL area with our rental car and when we arrived home we had a bill for $25 from the rental car company, followed six months later by a whopping 130 Euro bill from the Municipality of Florence." Had they read this book they would have noted the critical tip on the ZTL.

TIP> Avoiding driving accidently in the ZTL area and its costly fine.
Gee, some of the readers that purchased this book may know many of these tips. That's fine! However, if you pick-up one good tip this book has paid for itself. If you read this entire book you will find that it will pay for itself over and over.

If you know of any other tips and would like them to be included in the second edition of this book, please email me at thegelatopress@gmail.com (note you must include "the" in the email). I will certainly include them and give you a credit.

Many times in this book I will share a tip with you which not only pertains to travel in Italy but also pertains to travel in general. You should consider these general or extra tips as a "bonus".

TIP> What this book is not. If you are looking for a detailed "what to see and do" or the history of a particular town, city or site, this book will not provide that information. You need to pick up a detailed tour book on Italy or a specific book on the cities or regions you wish to see.

TIP> If you really want to plan your trip to Italy so there are no "oops" i.e. I could not see the Sistine Chapel or I had to take the train the next day and had only one day in Venice instead of two days, then you need to read this book.

You Need to Know Before You Go

And as a final point, a lot of you may read this book and say, I knew that and I knew that also. However, if you pick up one critical TIP, this book has paid for itself. Hopefully you will pick up many TIPs.

Some notes before you start reading:

FORMATTING
You will find my TIPs in bold "Verdana". I add further information and comments in bold "Garamond". It is just easier to read.

NOMENCLATURE
I have violated many of the rules of the Chicago Manual of Style. In this way you will find it much easier to read. For example instead of spelling out two hours to Siena, I just use 2 hours to Siena.

When it comes to money, I interchange dollars and Euros freely and many times round them off. Since many of us don't understand the metric system, I interchange kilometers and miles freely. Many times I will just state it's about 20 minutes up the GRA Autostrada. For simple conversion, figure a kilometer is just over a half mile (and a little more) and a Euro is about 10% (plus a little more) than a dollar. In summary, 20 kilometers is about 12 miles and 20 Euros is about $23.

You have already dreamed about a vacation in Italy, now let's plan it and do it with all my TIPs.

So here we go with the basics.

CHAPTER 1

PLANNING AND THE BASICS

It is difficult and costly to wake up three months prior and plan a trip to Italy. You need a minimum of 6-9 months. The first thing you need to do is block out the weeks you want to travel.

TIP> Avoid travel in July and August

July and August are beastly hot in Italy. In addition, Italy is packed with hordes and hordes of tourists. Avoid at all costs travelling in these two months. In addition if you are staying at a hotel in Rome, be advised that per city code hotels must turn the air-conditioning system off at midnight and coast till 6AM when they can turn it on again.

In addition, air fare is at a peak and so are hotel rates. Many restaurants in Rome are closed for two weeks for vacation during the month of August.

If you had any plans on a papal audience or seeing the Holy Father in St. Peter's Square on Sunday morning, forget it. Like everyone else, the Pope also gets away from the heat and retreats to his summer home at Castel Gandolffo in the cool hills of Frascati about 30 miles southwest of Rome.

TIP> The 330 day rule: If you are using your frequent flyer miles or points it is best to book 11 months prior. If you are not booking with frequent flyer miles see my TIPs under Air Fare Tips below.

Most of the major airlines operate on what is known as the 330 day rule (or the 11 month rule). This means that they load schedules into their computers only 330 days prior to the flight

You Need to Know Before You Go

date. If your airline will allow you to book the outbound leg, certainly do so. However, in most cases you will have to wait for the 330 days before your return trip. A few days here and there is not a big deal. I always book with the 330 day rule and get the best flights, utilize the least amount of frequent flyer points and pay the least amount of taxes. Here is what happens if you wake up about two months prior to you planned visit and want to use your frequent flyer points: It's a real case but, it is a fictitious airline. However, let's assume you live in New York City, this would be your routing.

JFK-DEN (Denver) - 5 hours
DEN-ORD (Chicago) 4 hours
ORD-LHR (London) - 8 hours
LHR-FCO (Rome)   - 3 hours
Hotel at Heathrow – next flight to Rome
  is in the morning, what?

And to boot:
80,000 miles per person.

I asked the agent "can't I just fly over to Chicago" she said "all the frequent flyer seats are gone", I have to give you this routing. In addition, that put me into London-Heathrow late in the day, however, the next flight to Rome (on their partner airline) wasn't until the following morning. So I had to find a room at one of those airport hotels and catch the flight to Rome first thing in the morning, oy, oy, oy.

Had I planned this trip 11 months out I would have used 40,000 miles per person and received the following routing:

JFK-FCO (Rome)   7 hours.

Stated in simplicity… "It's the early bird that gets the worm".

ITALY Over 300 Critical Tips

TIP> Before you book a fully escorted tour you should know the pros and cons.
Fully escorted tours do serve a purpose. I ran them for over 30 years. Just leave the driving to us. You usually get a seasoned tour guide who know the "ropes". You will learn a lot and usually have most everything included. You won't have to wait on long lines to see the Sistine Chapel and all those other sites.

However, they are extremely regimented. If you want to shop longer at the Nuovo Mercado in Florence, you won't be able to as you need to get on the bus (coach) by 5PM to go back to the hotel; which of course is not in Florence but in Montecatini Terme. See my write-up in the Florence chapter on where to stay and the benefits of staying at Montecatini Terme.

Escorted tours are pricy compared to making your own arrangements (known to travel agents as FIT, or Foreign Independent Travel). However, today with the internet you can make your own hotel, air and rail reservations. Many hotel booking websites allow you to cancel your reservation a week before or even closer to the check-in date (Booking.com).

Also, don't be fooled by low priced fully escorted tours. At the reception the first night you may be surprised that you will have to pay $300 more to participate in the evening dinner program. And, perhaps you will take that free day and go with the group to Naples and Pompeii with lunch of course. It's only an additional $249. If you have ever taken a cruise you will know that all these "shore" excursions can add up. Oh, don't miss the Rome by Night with dinner. It's only $189 extra per person!

In summary expect to pay more. Even if you don't want to drive with those "crazy" Italians you can still see pretty much everything in Italy by rail...even the minor sites i.e. Matera, the Lakes Region, etc.

You Need to Know Before You Go

TIP> You need a minimum of two weeks

Jet lag will do a number on your body. It is best to allow two weeks for your trip. Whether this is your first trip or a subsequent trip it is best to allow two weeks. This includes both fly days. So, you will net 12 days on the ground. If you are not doing an open jaw i.e. Fly into Rome and out of Venice or Milan you will need a day to get back to your return airport and you will need to put yourself up at an airport hotel the night before, else you chance missing your flight back home.

Here is a sample itinerary for first timers with a fly in and out of Rome. I discuss it at length in the itineraries chapter:

Day 1   Fly to Rome (overnight flight)
Day 2   Rome
Day 3   Rome
Day 4   Rome
Day 5   Rome to Florence morning train
Day 6   Florence
Day 7   Florence- Day Trip Pisa & Lucca
Day 8   Florence- Day Trip San Gimignano
Day 9   Florence- Day Trip Siena
Day 10 Morning train to Venice
Day 11 Venice
Day 12 Venice
Day 13 Train back to Rome- Overnight FCO apt
Day 14 Fly back to the USA

Now if you were lucky enough to book an "open-jaw" you would return from Venice. This would gain you another day. My suggestion is that you use this as an extra day in Florence for a day trip to the Cinque Terre.

You can use the excellent rail system of Italy or rent a car and drive. For more information on seeing the best of Italy by rail, order from Amazon my book *"ITALY the Best Places to See by Rail"*. It's also available in Kindle.

ITALY Over 300 Critical Tips

If you "short" the trip to 7-9 days the jet lag will really do a number on you. You need to figure that the day you arrive in Italy and check into your hotel from that grueling overnight flight, you will only have a few hours of sight-seeing in Rome. By 4PM all you want to do is take a nap! On Day 3 it gets a little better.

TIP> Know the six month rule with passports

I have a friend of mine. As a first timer, he checked in at the check in desk of an airline in Boston for a two week trip to Italy. He hadn't traveled outside the country for quite some time. He presented his passport to the agent only to find out that the airline would not board him. Why? Here's why: He was checking in on June 1. His passport was set to expire on July 1. His return flight from Rome was on June 12. The airline refused to board him stating the ninety day rule. He actually wanted to save the $110 fee for a new passport.

Here is the rule: For travel to most countries you need a passport expiration at least six months forward. There is a conflict with Italy as many websites state six months and some state three months. I am not sure why they have this. The only thing I can imagine is that if you were perhaps in an auto accident you could be hospitalized or in rehab for a period of at least six months and technically you would be in Italy without a valid passport for your return to the USA.

You need a valid passport for your return (mandated by the US government) and Italian authorities are under strict rules by the US Customs and Border Protection agency to not allow any US citizen to board a flight to the USA without a valid US passport.

TIP> Use the open jaw to see more

The best approach when visiting Italy is to use the open jaw approach. This eliminates back tracking to your arrival city and saves a day. You can usually fly in to the major cities of Italy i.e. Rome, Venice and Milan non-stop from the USA. However, as of this writing the major airlines do not fly non-stop to Naples, Pisa, Florence, Palermo or any of the minor cities in Italy. You will have to connect. However, consider flying into Rome, Venice and Milan and out of Rome, Venice and Milan. You can also fly into Pisa and out of Rome. However, these will require connections (transfers) in major cities of Europe. See the section below on airfare TIPs.

TIP> Use rail and eliminate the stress

For first timers, my suggestion is to use the ultra high speed rail system. Please do not compare this with the Amtrak of the USA. It is completely different. Imagine being whisked from Rome to Florence in about 90 minutes and at a cost of about $30 per person and $45 in first class. Using the rail system will eliminate the stress of driving on the Italian roads and it's in-expensive. In addition, it will save lots of time which will add to your sight-seeing experience.

TIP> Consider a combination of rail and car

This is another stress eliminator. You travel by rail between the major cities and then rent a car and do the countryside. Most major train stations (Staziones) have rental car facilities just like the airport. So you can visit Rome then travel by rail to Florence. After seeing Florence you rent a car at the Santa Maria Novella train station in Florence and travel around the wine country of Chianti (about 20 miles south of Florence) for perhaps five days. It's best to return the car to the Florence rail station then continue your journey to Venice. See my chapter on Driving a Car in Italy.

ITALY Over 300 Critical Tips

----- AIR FARE TIPS ------

TIP> You will find the least expensive fares to Italy in the winter and the shoulder seasons April & May and mid October to mid December. This is called the "low" season.
If you want to spend $1200 round trip (coach) to Italy for the second week of June, buy your tickets in April. However if you want to save money and you are not using frequent flyer miles, visit Italy in the low season as stated above. Once you determine that you will visit in the low season, you can buy your tickets anytime. You can figure $500-700 per person on a non-refundable ticket.

TIP> Before blocking out a 10 day or two week period of time, check to see that you are not travelling in any holiday period.
You can easily check this out on the internet. Take a look at events at the Vatican. If you are originating your travel, say four days before Easter, you may not be able to get a decent hotel in Rome or even a hotel room at all! Avoid any major holiday period where hotel rooms may be scarce or at a premium. Not only does this apply to events in Rome, but also to events and festivals in Venice, Florence and Siena.

There are other problems associated with holiday or festival travel times. Many times the "preferred" trains will be fully booked and often major attractions will be extremely crowded.

TIP> For rock bottom fares consider an on-line subscription to SCOTTS CHEAP FLIGHTS.
If I told you I could fly to Italy for $289 round trip from most major US cities, would you believe it? Well you can and it's easy to do.

10

You Need to Know Before You Go

First before I discuss Scottscheapflights let me give you the conditions of that $289 fare:

1. It's definitely a low season fare. Don't expect to fly the second week of July or the last week in June. However, you need not go in January either.
2. Most airlines have these rock-bottom fares called "basic economy". What this means is they will charge you for your bags. It will run about $40-60 per flight. So you can figure about $120-240 more for your bags.
3. Bear in mind that basic economy is not available on all flights. It's what I call a promo fare or a "tickler" fare. Many airlines will offer it hoping you will pay for the bags and the seat assignment. But you know better!
4. There is no seat assignment when you make your reservation. You will get your seats when you check in for the flight.

TIP> Use carry-on bags and avoid bag fees.

TIP> Arrive at least three hours early; inform the agent that you are travelling with someone else and they will do their best to seat you together.
If you cannot be seated together or across the aisle best idea is when you board the plane ask another person if they would swap seats with you so you can be next to your partner.

TIP> Check the airline rules. Many of the major airlines are allowing seat selection on basic economy to be made 24 hours prior. This cuts down on seat selection time at the check-in counter.
However, bear in mind you may have to pay for your large bags unless you have carry-on bags. Yes, those small roller bags (rollies) and those carry on back-packs.

Now, how do you get that $289 fare? Simple, you need to be notified when a tickler fare, a mistake fare or a basic economy fare is available. I recommend Scottscheapflights.com unless you want to be checking your favorite airline each day. Scotts uses what is known as "push technology". Instead of checking their website each and every day, they send you the information in accordance with your profile.

You can check out the website and it's free. However, I would strongly suggest that you pay the $39 per year and get notified when the fare is available.

Now, don't panic yet. You don't fly on an airline known as Scott's Airline, or any obscure airline or any charter airline. They are all the airlines we all know: Alitalia, Delta, American, British Air, Lufthansa, etc. Scott is nothing more than what I call a "bird-dogger". He only points you to the airline having that $289 deal. You still need to go to the airline's website, book it and then pay for it.

Once you are notified you must book that fare on-line with the respective airline in a hurry, like immediately or within 24 hours, else it will be gone. You need to be ready to "strike" as soon as the fare becomes available. Remember, these fares can be announced 6-9 months out.

Once paying your $39 per year fee, you will get all announcements. You also need to fill out your profile. Since I live in Boston, I fill out my profile and specify that I can fly out of Boston or New York.

Here is a typical email from Scotts Cheap Flights:

TO: ROME
Boston (BOS) $246 (non-stop)
Burbank (BUR) $264
Los Angeles (LAX) $264 (non-stop
Ontario (ONT) $264
Santa Ana (SNA) $264

You Need to Know Before You Go

AIRLINES:
Air Canada
Lufthansa
United
Alitalia

WHEN:
November through May;
Late August through September;
Includes Thanksgiving but no Christmas or New Years.

PURCHASE BY:
These fares will last 1-2 days. This is Scott's opinion.

Now, no wasting time here. You must immediately go to one of the airlines website's mentioned and book it directly.

Remember these fares are usually not refundable. However, many airlines will allow you to cancel the reservation and will hold your funds for up to one year in hopes that you will use them within the one year period. Rebooking fees may apply.

TIP> Check other fare cities for open jaw returns i.e. fly into Rome or Milan and out of Naples, etc.
Many times Scotts publishes a "Europe on Sale" fare. These usually occur 6-9 months in advance.

TIP> Don't jump at the first fare Scotts announces unless it meets your exact requirements.
What I mean by the above is that if you find 9 months out an exact "city pair" fare i.e. fly into Rome and out of Venice says for $320 on basic economy, then book it and pay for it. However, don't compromise too early in the game. In other words, if there is an extremely low fare in and out of Zurich on Swiss Air, you can always hop an in-expensive flight to Rome and also on the return from Venice or wherever. Consider, also taking the train OVER the Alps to or from Switzerland and

extending your trip a few days. I devote an entire chapter to this on my rail book of Italy.

Also remember that these discount fares may come up every few weeks. So you need not grab the first one. However, if it fits the bill... go for it!

CHAPTER 2

ITINERARIES

How this chapter is organized: First I describe the TIPs associated with the suggested Classic 10 day visit for first timers to Italy. I include Day 1 and Day 10 which are fly days as part of the ten days. Yes, this is a "compressed" trip with just the minimal amount of time to visit the most important sites, and yes, eat great pasta and all that good stuff.

After I discuss the TIPs associated with the Classic 10 Day Trip, which can also be done in reverse i.e. start in Venice an end in Rome, I discuss TIPs associated with extensions to the Amalfi area before starting your visit to Rome and an extension to Milan to visit the Lakes District after visiting Venice.

You should take note as some of the TIPs are associated with day trips from Florence. These day trips i.e. Pisa, Lucca, The Cinque Terre, Siena, San Gimignano, etc. will add more days to your visit to Florence.

Throughout this book you will find references to driving the itinerary or taking the train or a combination of both. Do not compare train travel in Italy to our Amtrak (or Via Rail in Canada). They are worlds apart.

TIP> After you block out your outbound and inbound air you need to consider certain restrictions. You may need to slightly adjust your fly days to take into account these restrictions, additional days in Florence and/or the extensions to Amalfi and Milan (The Lakes District).

ITALY Over 300 Critical Tips

TIP> It may be better to plan the trip first and then block out the air arrangements.
Before I give you tips on certain restrictions you need to know some of the suggested itineraries for your trip so here they are:

ROME-FLORENCE-VENICE – THE CLASSIC 10
This is the classic first timer trip to Italy. It has the minimum time you will need of ten days, including the fly days:

Classic 10 Day Suggested Itinerary
Day 1 - Fly to Rome
Day 2 – Arrive Rome – recovery day
Day 3- Rome – Monumental day
Day 4- Rome- The Vatican
Day 5- Morning train to Florence
Day 6- Florence
Day 7- Florence
Day 8- Morning train to Venice
Day 9- Venice
Day 10- Fly home from Venice

From now on I will refer to this itinerary as the Classic Ten Day visit, sometimes known as the Three Capitals Tour. You can extend the Three Capitals itinerary by adding days. Please see below for the Itinerary Extensions.

--------- ROME AND THE VATICAN --------

TIP> On arrival in Rome, hopefully between 7AM and 2PM; if you are not suffering from severe jetlag, consider one of the Hop-on-Hop-off buses for an orientation tour of Rome.
Using one of these buses will provide you with an overview of the historic district, also known as the Centro Historico. Try not to get on and off all the time since visiting an attraction will

take a considerable amount of time and you will be forced to wait for the next bus to come around. In fact, if it was me I would not even get off the bus for two hours. The basic cost is about $15 with the audio package it's $25 and well worth it.

TIP> It is best to take a 4 hour city tour without The Vatican or the Coliseum

I strongly recommend this if you are not doing a hop-on-hop off type of orientation tour. Don't confuse this with the Hop-on-Hop-off bus. This is a four hour city tour. The Vatican consumes an awful lot of time and is best done on a separate day. Please see my write-up under The Vatican. However, if you can get a city tour which includes the Coliseum and the Forum it will pay off. You get the tickets included and an expert guide and usually 3 or 4 visits i.e. Trevi Fountain, Pantheon, etc.

Also, you should note that the government of Italy has mandated in most historical areas the use of audio units. These units are supplied on all tours. Your tour director will speak into a microphone and broadcast to your audio unit.

TIP> It is best to plan your tours and pay for them on-line before you go. If you arrive in Rome, check into your hotel and ask the concierge or the desk clerk to set up your tour, many times they will insist on cash since they will take their commission out of it. You will pay the same amount whether you book on-line or pay at the hotel however, most times you will not be able to use your credit card at the hotel. The tours tend to be pricy and at this point you may not even have Euros with you.

TIP> Most four hour tours have a morning tour and an afternoon tour. Check the times on-line before you buy and do not "short" the time. If a tour starts at 9AM and your flight arrives in Rome at

7AM it will be tight to make the 9AM tour. Best would be to book the afternoon tour which usually starts around 3PM. This will also help you if your flight is delayed.

TIP> If you want to attend a Papal Audience, Day 1 must be a Monday.
Papal Audience's are giving only on Wednesday mornings in the special Papal Auditorium abutting St. Peter's Square. Do not confuse this with the Papal Angelus which is given at 10 or 11AM each Sunday in St. Peter's Square. This is where the Pope appears from the window of his apartment and blesses the massive crowd in St. Peters.

The Papal Audience is completely different. The auditorium holds about 2,000 people. Many seats are reserved. The invited guests (you) arrive about an hour before the Holy Father. Groups from all over the world arrive and sing songs. At 10AM the Pope arrives with all that pomp and circumstance. He delivers a speech in several languages and blesses all. On certain Wednesdays the audience takes places in St. Peter's Square. Take it from me, even if you are not Catholic attending a Papal Audience is quite impressive and moving. In addition, it's free. I personally attended one in 1972.

In order to attend a Papal Audience contact your local Catholic Priest or your local Arch Diocese or request them from the Vatican directly. If you fly on a Monday, you arrive on a Tuesday and you will be able to attend the Papal Audience on Wednesday. There is absolutely no charge for tickets. And further, if anyone tries to sell you tickets they are probably counterfeit! You should watch out for scammers.

TIP> If you want to visit the Sistine Chapel and the Vatican Museum you must purchase tickets before you leave the USA, else wait on a line for 2-3 hours.

You Need to Know Before You Go

If you arrive in Rome and want to visit the Vatican Museum and view the ceiling of the Sistine Chapel painted by Michelangelo in 1512, you must purchase your tickets as soon as they go on sale. If you do not do this you will wait on a line about one half mile long. Trust me on this one.

The line forms outside the walls of the Vatican (The Holy See, an independent country from Italy) about 7AM. It is four to six people deep. They will wait 2-3 hours before they can buy their tickets, pass security and enter the main gallery.

TIP> The Vatican Museum and its Sistine Chapel are only open Monday through Saturday. However, they are open the last Sunday of the month with a shorter closing time, not recommended.

TIP> Purchase your Vatican Museum ticket's directly on-line from the Vatican Museum's official website (Museivaticani.va) to realize the best price instead of ticket brokers and tour operators who will charge you a premium.
You may charge with your credit card, but make sure you have your credit card that you used on you when entering the Vatican Museum. Tickets are issued for time slots. On a given day over 30,000 people visit the museum.

TIP> If you time your stay in Rome properly you can attend a Papal Audience on Wednesday at 10AM, have lunch on the Borgo Pio and then visit the museum at 3PM.

TIP> There are so many restaurants around the Vatican you will not have any problem finding one. Also, note that unlike many tourist places in Italy the prices on the menu are extremely reasonable. There are well over 50 restaurants on the Borgo Pio and its side streets. When leaving St. Peter's

Square (not the Museum) just bear to your left, walk three blocks and take a hard right and you will be on the Borgo Pio. You should note that most of the eateries are between St. Peter's and the Museum entrance located about 12 blocks away to your left. There are very few eateries on the right as you exit St. Peter's Square.

TIP> If you have any plans on visiting the Coliseum and the Roman Forum, it's best to purchase your tickets on-line. Several days of the year there is free admission. Best to check the official website at coopculture.it (yes, it sounds odd but this is the official website).

You Need to Know Before You Go

------------FLORENCE------------
"FIRENZE" IN ITALIAN

TIP> Before visiting Florence, it is best to obtain your tickets to the Accademia and the Uffizi Gallery. You will wait on line at the Accademia to see Michelangelo's David at least two hours before you are allowed in to purchase your tickets. If you plan on visiting the Uffizi, you won't find a line there. You must arrive with prepaid tickets. Electronic signs advise visitors when the next date and time tickets are available. I call these the "Shutout Signs". In other words you are shut out of a visit until you see something posted on these signs.

TIP> If you are visiting Florence for two days, you should take note that the Accademia featuring Michelangelo's "David" is closed on Mondays. Also, the Uffizi Gallery housing the masterpieces of art from the Renaissance is also closed. There are several appointed agencies which sell tickets and tours for the Accademia. You can buy tickets for the Uffizi Gallery at Uffizi.it.

TIP> You can do both the Accademia to view the David and visit the Uffizi Gallery in one day.
It is rather difficult to visit both museums on arrival in Florence. Even if you drive and care not to take the high-speed train (the Frecci's) it will be a rush, rush, rush.

The best approach is to leave your arrival day for taking it easy in Florence. Visit the magnificent Duomo (the Cathedral) with its pink and green marble, it's free. Then have lunch in Piazza Signoria; follow up with a visit to the Nuovo Mercado (inexpensive shopping) and finally end your day with shopping or people watching on the Ponte Vecchio bridge.

ITALY Over 300 Critical Tips

On the following day, assuming it's not a Monday, visit the Accademia arriving 10-11AM. View the David, spend some time viewing the other exhibits and on your way out stop at the book store. You will need one hour here.

About the noon hour stroll over to the Piazza Signoria for lunch. Then about 2-3PM visit the Uffizi Gallery located only about two blocks from the Piazza Signoria.

TIP> See my tips on being Street Savvy in the Security Chapter. All of these tourist attractions are targets for pickpockets, especially the Ponte Vecchio Bridge area.

You Need to Know Before You Go

------ FLORENCE EXTENSIONS ----
PISA AND LUCCA

TIP> You can visit Pisa and the medieval city of Lucca on your first or second day in Florence.
This is great on a Monday when the Accademia and the Uffizi are closed. There are two approaches, one is an early morning train out of Rome's Termini station ...Yikes, I can't get up that early and miss that great Italian breakfast. So the better approach is to take an evening train on Day 4. It is only a 90 minute fast run to Florence on one of the Frecci trains operated by the state run railway company "Trenitalia" or the independent company Italo. I would suggest a train around 8PM. Remember to purchase your ticket before you leave the USA as many late trains and morning trains are heavily booked.

If you are driving, it is a little more complex. See my write-up in the chapter "Driving in Italy".

Suggest you purchase your Panini at the Termini rail station before you leave. That same Panini will cost you twice as much on the train!

Here is how you do it. On arrival at Florence's Santa Maria Novella train station about 9:30PM or 10PM, either walk over to your hotel if you just have carry-ons or take a taxi for about 5-7 Euros to your hotel. Remember always to ask the driver about how much it will cost, first. Check into your hotel.

The next morning go back to the Santa Maria Novella station at 10-11AM and buy a ONE WAY ticket to Pisa Centrale. I say one way because you will not be returning to Florence via Pisa. You will return via Lucca. See tips on how to buy rail tickets under the chapter "Rail Travel in Italy".

ITALY Over 300 Critical Tips

In less than one hour you will arrive in Pisa. On exiting the train, just follow the crowd. They are all going to the same place. It is about a half mile walk. If you care not to walk you can take a taxi for about 5-7Euros or a bus.

There is no entrance fee for the Leaning Tower complex.

TIP> On the streets abutting the Tower complex you will find lots and lots of street vendors selling fake Gucci's and Rolex's. Many of these vendors are a decoy for their buddies running "pick and run". So when you are looking at those fake watches and handbags, hold on to your wallet (keep your hand in your pocket) and ladies keep that zipper closed on your handbag and make sure you clutch it.

TIP> If you want to climb the Leaning Tower (not recommended for seniors) you can purchase tickets on-line at several websites. It's about $15-20 per person plus booking and credit card fees. I might note you will still have to queue up on the line, even with a ticket. If you want to climb the tower you must figure two hours! This will eat in to your time if you want to go to Lucca.

TIP> You can easily visit the medieval city of Lucca in the afternoon and it's only 30 minutes from Pisa.
Here is how you do it. I strongly suggest leaving Pisa about 1PM and heading for Lucca. If you have ever been to a medieval walled city this one is a gem. And, best of all you don't have to climb a hill and huff and puff to get there. The town is flat and the rail station is just across the street from the main gates into the town. If you are a fan of opera you should note that Lucca is the birthplace of Puccini. You will find shops everywhere selling Puccini souvenirs.

You Need to Know Before You Go

Check before you leave the USA on Trenitalia.com for the train schedule from Pisa to Lucca. There are trains to Lucca every 30 minutes. The cost is about $4 and it takes about 25 minutes. You need only purchase a ONE WAY ticket, since you will return to Florence via a different rail line (Florence-Via Reggio line). Remember to validate that ticket on the platform at Pisa.

TIP> On arrival in Lucca, cross the street, enter the main gates, find that place to have a light lunch and perhaps a glass of local wine.

TIP> You need only buy your regional ticket at the rail station beforehand. No need to buy them online. There is a train every hour back to Florence Santa Maria Novella stazione. Most of the trains do the run in 1:20 minutes. However, many take longer and you will pay the same price, 8 Euros.

TIP> It is difficult and I have found it a hassle to do both Pisa and Lucca in one day by car. Best is to leave your car in the garage in Florence and just rail it for the day. It's fast, cheap and.... no stress.
If you decide to drive, it will take you about an hour just to get lost in Florence and head over to the Autostrada in the middle of rush hour. Hopefully, you will not enter any of the ZTL areas and risk a stiff fine; surprise, surprise, surprise when you arrive home. Secondly, out of Florence there are many Autostradas going in all directions. Assuming you are heading to Pisa you will have to contend with the tolls. On arrival in Pisa you must park your car about a half mile from the Leaning Tower complex. No need to worry here as they do provide a tram type service (like Universal Studios) that will take you over to the Leaning Tower complex. It runs every 10-15 minutes.

If you are driving, and after visiting Pisa you must work your way over to Lucca. Here is where the fun and stress comes in. You can't park inside the city walls. So, you need to find a parking area and then a parking meter. Pay your fee then walk into the town. Oh, and make sure you have enough money on the meter. The Policia will be watching all those meters.

It's not a big deal taking your car. It's just the stress and further it will add 2-3 hours to your day. Better to do a rail trip for the day and relax!

You Need to Know Before You Go

------ FLORENCE EXTENSION ---- SAN GIMIGNANO AND SIENA

TIP> If you have the time, I always recommend adding an extra day while in Florence, to visit the medieval towns/cities of San Gimignano and Siena.

TIP> Consult the internet for full day coach tours to both cities. Do remember that the coach tours are highly regimented.

I remember one year having pizza in Siena at an outdoor café on the main square, Piazza d Campo (it's not really a square) and the folks next to us had to get their pizza in a hurry to go, gulp down their wine since their coach was leaving for San Gimignano in 10 minutes.

TIP> If you want to visit these two cities you can easily do so via rail and yes in one day without the regimentation, and it's not a lot of money compared to the highly regimented escorted coach tour.

Here is how you do it. After breakfast, walk over to Florence Santa Maria Novella station and get a train about 9AM to Siena. All of the trains are pretty much local but the run is a fast 90 minutes and about 10 Euros.

On arrival in Siena make your way via the new escalator system to the old city. Enjoy walking and shopping on the old narrow streets, visiting the Duomo and then having lunch on the Piazza d Campo.

About 2PM, find your way back to the stazione and purchase a ticket to Poggibonsi-San Gimignano. It's about 30 minutes and less than 4 Euros. Make sure you board a train out of Siena bound for Florence (Firenze). As you exit the Poggibonsi-San Gimignano stazione, follow the crowd to the bus for the 20 minute ride to the main parking lot of San Gimignano.

ITALY Over 300 Critical Tips

Once in the main parking lot where the rest-rooms are, follow the crowd around the supermarket and café (good place to use the restrooms) and enter the main gates of this UNESCO World Heritage site. It is best to read up on this before your visit and understand what the towers of San Gimignano are all about.

TIP> If you are a lover of gelato like we are, you will find the best gelato in all of Italy (and possibly the best in the world) in San Gimignano.
The gelato shop is right in the center of the square. As you enter the square look directly to your left and you will notice the long line waiting to be served at Gelateria Dondoli. Dondoli whips up his own flavors in addition to all those "standard" flavors i.e. chocolate, lemon, etc.

About 5-6PM after your gelato, and collecting a bag of regional goodies i.e. Salumi (Salami) follow the crowd to the parking area and board that municipal bus for the 20 minutes back to the rail station for your one hour trip to Florence. It will cost you about 8 Euros. By the way, if you have seen the movie *Tea With Mussolini*, swing into the La Cisterna Hotel and take a look at the lobby where they filmed the movie.

Don't worry about taking a snooze on the train, the last stop will be Florence Santa Maria Novella stazione and you will be forced to wake up else you will go back to Siena!

Also with all train travel make sure you read the chapter Rail Travel Through Italy.

You Need to Know Before You Go

-----FLORENCE EXTENSION ----
THE CINQUE TERRE

TIP> Here is another tip if you can afford another day in Florence.   Take a trip to the Cinque Terre for the day. The Cinque Terre is the home of the five towns.   These towns were inaccessible until the Italian State Railway (known as FS) blasted tunnels through the mountains which hug the Ligurian Sea.

TIP> It is difficult and nearly impossible to visit the Cinque Terre if you are driving. You must still have to make your way to the main rail station at La Spezia and take the train about 10 minutes to the first town known as Riomaggorie.
Even if you drive it is difficult (unless you are a billy goat) to navigate the hills of the towns and find parking.

TIP> If you drive to La Spezia you will find it impossible to park your car at the station. It is best to park 6-10 blocks from the station and walk over. Make sure there are no visible valuables in your car. No problem here, there is a train every 20 minutes.

TIP> Do not get fooled by any policeman who says "just give me 20 Euros and I will let you park here" (at the station). By the time you get back, you will have a ticket and the policemen who gave you permission to park at the station will be long gone.

TIP> At most, you will be only able to visit two town's of the Cinque Terre. You will have to get an early start.   Best is to consult the internet on the five towns and then the Trenitalia website. Also note that Trenitalia has a ticket which allows you to visit all the five towns without buying individual rail tickets. Once again consult Trenitalia.com

Best is to hop a train to Riomaggiore (Town One) or better Manarola (Town Two) from Santa Maria Novella in Florence about 10AM; the fare is only 17 Euros (one way). It takes a little over 2.5 hours. After you have visited Riomaggiore, you need to buy a ticket for about one Euro to the next town which is Manarola. See my note on the all day tickets.

TIP> As of this writing the famous walk "Via Della Amore" (The Walk of the Lover's) between Riomaggiore and Manarola is still closed due to a land slide several years ago. Therefore, you must take the train (it's only 3 minutes) between the two towns. If you want to take a hike on steep paths between these two towns there are detailed maps available at most shops and the rail station tourist information booth. You should figure one hour.

TIP> You can also catch a train to the Cinque Terre from several other stations in Florence. So, there is no need to go back to Santa Maria Novella if you are walking distance to a closer station. The fare to Town One (Riomaggiore) or Town Two (Manarola) (and the other three towns) is the same from any station in the Florence area.

You should note that Santa Maria Novella has many more trains each day than the other stations.

TIP> If you have time to only visit one town, my suggestion is to visit Manarola. Why? Only because it's my favorite, and do have lunch at the Marina Piccola overlooking the sea if you are into seafood and great pasta.

TIP> This is a big TIP. Since it takes a little over 2.5 hours by train to reach the five towns, my

You Need to Know Before You Go

suggestion is to visit the Cinque Terre and spend the night there. This allows you to see all five towns by rail, since driving is quite difficult.

Here is how you do it. My suggestion is to leave your baggage in your room in Florence and pack a small "day bag" with just a change of underwear, your tooth brush, and your meds. See if your hotel in Florence will allow you to check in and out and store your bags in the baggage room while you are gone for the night. This will save you the charge for the hotel night in Florence. You then book a bed and breakfast in one of the five towns. There are no large hotels (or even small hotels) there.

You should remember that Italian law dictates that you must have your passport on you at all times while in Italy. Do not put your passport in that small day bag. Also, remember that it will be difficult to take a "rollie" type carry-on bag with you unless you can arrive at your selected bed and breakfast and check that rollie first. Also, if you are departing back to Florence from one of the other towns, you will be forced back to that bed and breakfast to retrieve your rollie.

I find that a small carryon bag or better a backpack is the way to go. You are now ready to enjoy that no-stress overnight visit to the Cinque Terre.

ITALY Over 300 Critical Tips

----- VENICE AND VENICE MESTRE -----

TIP> If you leave Florence late in the afternoon, early evening, or early morning via train you will arrive in a little over 2 hours in Venice. There is no need to take a mid-day train and miss an entire day of sightseeing. Both Trenitalia and Italo run very high speed trains between both cities.

TIP> It is best is to arrive at the Santa Maria Novella stazione early and get some food to go. It's a normal thing in Italy. Most of the people buying those pre-made sandwiches on the train will be tourists who did not read this book. The smart ones will be downing their caprese salads and their Panini's which they purchased for about half the price in the station and, don't forget the water.

TIP> If your visit to Venice is for only one or two days, you may want to stay in Venice Mestre (Mestre rhymes with "pastry"). When most people speak of Venice they are talking about the world famous Lagoon area. Venice Mestre is the mainland part of Venice. The hotels in Venice Mestre are dramatically less expensive than the hotels in the Lagoon. Many times staying in the Venice Lagoon becomes a logistical nightmare, as I discuss below.
In Mestre, you will find numerous modern hotels as opposed to the hotels which line the canals of Venice and are quite old, but quaint. Many of the modern hotels are located in Mestre opposite the Venice Mestre train station. My favorite is the four star Plaza Hotel. This is an excellent four star hotel for about $120-150 per night including breakfast. If you book directly (recommended), do give my best regards to Maurizio the General Manager.

You Need to Know Before You Go

There is a train to Venice Santa Lucia station, in the lagoon, which is the end of the rail line, every 15-20 minutes. So, if you stay at one of these hotels all you need do is hop the train for about $1.50 and you will be at the Grand Canal in about 12 minutes. Practically all trains bound for Venice from all over Italy and Europe stop at Venice Mestre and then continue on to the Santa Lucia terminal in the Lagoon.

There are also numerous hotels in Mestre which are not opposite the train station but allow easy access to the Venice Lagoon via buses which make stops every 15 minutes in front of most hotels. Several hotels have their own shuttle buses which will take you directly to the Grand Canal and drop you at the Piazzale Roma which is the end of the causeway.

TIP> You can only board Regional Trains at Mestre going into the Lagoon. Do not attempt to board the Frecci or Italo high speed reserved seat trains or better the Simplon Orient Express. These trains will only discharge passengers at Mestre.

TIP> If you are driving between the two cities i.e. Florence and Venice, it will take you a good 4 hours including stops. It's an easy trip. However, it may consume an entire half day. Do consider staying in Mestre as there is plenty of paid parking right opposite the Mestre train station for about $18 per day. It's about the same price you will pay at those big garages to the right of the Piazzale Roma as you enter the Lagoon area.

TIP> There are also other large hotels in the Mestre area which are not opposite the train station. Consult your favorite booking engine for more information and courtesy shuttles if you are arriving by train. Most charge for parking.

ITALY Over 300 Critical Tips

TIP> If you stay in Mestre, you won't have to port your bags around the canals and over bridges which can be difficult.
However, staying in the Lagoon does have its advantages. First, no question the place is very romantic. Second, it is unique seeing all those boats running up and down the canals and third if you are a senior you can take a nap before dinner.

TIP> Unless you are arriving with carry-on baggage, consider hiring a porter at Santa Lucia station or at the main parking garage to transport your bags and find your hotel.
Venice is a maze with over 400 bridges connecting all those islands (there are about 120) in the Lagoon. In addition add on negotiating all those bridges and you will have one hell of an experience. And yes, you will have to dodge hordes of people, many on small alleys.

TIP> Ask the porter how much it will cost you to bring you to your hotel with your bags. Rates run about 25-50 Euros per couple. Rates usually do not vary since Venice is made up of several districts and the porter's prices are based on which district you are going to.

TIP> Ask the porter if you will have to travel to your hotel via the Vaporetto (one of the water buses) and further does the rate include the tickets to the Vaporetto?
Many porters will get you to your hotel using one of the Vaporettos (Vaporetti). Be aware that he may ask you for another $25 to purchase Vaporetto tickets or he may request you to purchase the tickets for you and the porter at the black and yellow Vaporetto ticket booth.

You Need to Know Before You Go

You can figure 30-60 minutes to escort you and your bags to your hotel. You need not tip the porter. Your quoted price is it. Also, the porters only take cash as in Euros. It is best if you do not have Euros by now that you find an ATM (cash point) at the train station or the airport. Best ones to use are labeled "BANCOMAT". See my Chapter on Money and Credit Cards.

You should note that if you are staying in the Lagoon and flying home from Venice's Marco Polo airport, you need to figure at least 90 minutes to get over to the Piazzale Roma in order to hop in a taxi or the bus for a 30 minute ride to Marco Polo.

TIP> If you want to stay in the Lagoon area and don't want to navigate some of those massive bridges like the one opposite the train station "Ponte degli Scalzi" (it's on the left as you come down all those steps from the station) best is to stay at a hotel to the left of the train station. There is no need to cross the Grand Canal; and you will find the bridges you have to negotiate, quite small. However, best is to use the services of a porter. Don't worry, there are plenty of them once you exit the train station. Look for the gents wearing nice blue coveralls (or jumpsuits). I have not seen any woman porter's yet in those blue jumpsuits but keep looking.

TIP> You need not drag your bags down all those steps at the station. If you exit the train platform, look to your left and you will notice an exit. This leads to a path down to the base of those steps.

TIP> The restrooms are also located to the left of the platforms as you exit the train, and you will need to bring a one Euro coin with you. There is usually an attendant who will make change for you.

ITALY Over 300 Critical Tips

TIP> Consult the internet for your days in Venice or contact the hotel via email. If there will be "Alta Aqua" you should bring a pair of light weight boots. Venice floods in these times and even though the Alta Aqua brigade does its best to put out those planks of wood over the flooded areas, you will probably still get your feet wet. If you don't have boots (they may be quite heavy to pack in your luggage) I suggest those one gallon baggies you buy in the supermarket and a few rubber bands to place around your ankles. They work great as improvised Venice Alta Aqua boots.

TIP> As a final tip, if you are staying in Mestre at the train station hotels, you will find an excellent restaurant about three blocks behind the Hotel Plaza. It is called "Da Bepi"; absolutely great seafood and not expensive. Do tell "The Brothers" that you learned of their restaurant from Bob at National Travel Vacations who sent them the Boston Red Sox hats and the Patriots T-shirts! They will make sure you get an extra dish of great olives.

I discuss more tips on Venice in my Chapter on Venice.

You Need to Know Before You Go

----- ITINERARY EXTENSION ----
NAPLES, POMPEII AND AMALFI
BEFORE ROME

TIP> You can visit Naples and the Amalfi coast two different ways: Begin your visit to Italy by flying into Naples instead of Rome. Or fly into Rome and take the one hour train down to Naples. There are 1-2 trains every hour operated by Trenitalia or Italo. The fast train makes the journey in about one hour and ten minutes and costs about 20 Euros.

Here are your extra days:

Day 2 Fly into Naples or Rome and rail down to Napoli. Note, Day 2 is not really an extra day since it is your arrival day, same as Day 2 in Rome. You won't be able to do much except get some rest at your hotel in Sorrento (recommended) see below.

Amalfi Day 3 The Island of Capri

Amalfi Day 4 Day trip to Pompeii and Shopping in Sorrento

Amalfi Day 5 The Amalfi Drive and Positano

TIP> Take note on the above days and arrange your Amalfi Day 3 to be your Capri day.

If for some reason there are rough seas, the ferries to Capri will not run. If this is the case, it is best to visit Capri as Day 4 or 5.

TIP> Suggest you do not stay in Naples, but go directly to Sorrento, it is easier to do the day trips, safer and yes...nicer.

Once you arrive at the main rail station on Garibaldi Square you need to follow the signs to the Circumvisuviana Railway. Purchase your ticket from the machine for Sorrento (about 5 Euros) and in an hour you will arrive at the last stop... Sorrento. Note you must take a train marked "Sorrento".

On arrival in Sorrento find your hotel; most of the time you can walk there or take a taxi for less than 7 Euros and enjoy that well deserved nap. I suggest Sorrento because it can be used as a base for day trips to Positano, Capri and the ruins of Pompeii.

TIP> To view the ruins of Pompeii which were buried in more than six feet of ash and pumice when Mount Vesuvius erupted in 79AD, all you need do is hop the same train from Sorrento station in the direction of Napoli (Naples). At Sorrento it only goes one way since it is the end of the line, so no need to worry.
Suggest you leave Sorrento about 10AM. It's about 50 minutes to Pompeii and the entrance is just across from the rail station. Yes, they will take your credit card and you need not purchase your tickets ahead of time. Pompeii is absolutely mind boggling and it is humongous. It's the remains of a city about twenty times the size of the Roman Forum. What's most interesting is that Pompeii was only discovered in 1869. In fact, many of the buildings are still being unearthed. You will need a good 2-3 hours here. Afterwards enjoy a lunch at many of the cafes and restaurants . Hotel MEC Pizzeria is one of the best.

Take the train back to Sorrento and enjoy the shopping on the back streets. Take a nap and have dinner at one of my favorite places....Da Filippo. You should note that Da Filippo will pick you up at your hotel and bring you back at no charge. Have your hotel desk clerk or the concierge call Da Filippo for a reservation and a courtesy pickup. And remember to tip the driver a couple of Euros.

TIP> Visit the island of Capri on your second day on the Amalfi coast. Have your concierge check the schedule and walk over (and down) to the Marina Piccola for your 30 minute fast catamaran to the Island of Capri. On arrival take the funicular to the top of the old city and check out the shopping and the real wealthy people (the "A" list crowd). Enjoy lunch and more shopping and then head back to

You Need to Know Before You Go

Sorrento (not Naples or Positano) late in the day. If you spot the paparazzi racing around, do ask who they are chasing. I am sure it will be someone famous, perhaps an actress or a "supermodel".

TIP> On arrival in Capri, and just as you walk off the pier, you will be approached by the "Blue Grotto hawker's". The Blue Grotto is a water filled cave accessed only by the sea. You should read up on this in the tour books since the biggest complaint is that you will need to take a small boat up to the cave, about 30 minutes, and then perhaps wait 30-60 minutes to board another smaller boat which will take you into the grotto. There are land tours to the Blue Grotto, however, you must still board a boat to enter it. Do check the reviews.

TIP> The Island of Capri is split into two areas: Capri and Anacapri. In addition to those Blue Grotto hawker's there are drivers who will take you on a 2-4 hour tour of the island. You should note that no cars are allowed in the old city of Capri. In addition, hotels (mostly B&B's) are far less expensive in Anacapri. However, you will need to take the bus or a taxi to the old city for shopping, etc. It's not a big deal as Capri is only 2 miles away.

TIP> If you are not going to the Blue Grotto by boat or taking a tour of the island by taxi, you will need to exit the pier area to purchase tickets for the funicular which will take you up to the old city. You will find the ticket booth to your right. The cost is about 4 Euros per person and yes you can use your credit card. If you care not to take the funicular, you can certainly walk the switchbacks with all the shops, but it is a real huff and puff. Suggest saving it for the walk back to the marina area, since it will

be all downhill. You should allow plenty of time, at least an hour, before your catamaran's scheduled trip back to the Sorrento Marina Piccola.

TIP> On your return to Sorrento, there is an elevator (lift) which will take you from the Marina Piccola to the small park right off the Piazza Tasso. If you are "bushed" and don't want to take that long walk up the hill (Oy, it's a real long walk) or climb that giant staircase, then take the lift. It will probably be the best 2 Euros you have ever spent.

It is sometimes difficult to locate the lift. Best is to ask someone on exiting the pier area and not a tourist "Dov'e e escinsor" (Dough Vey Escinsor)?

You should note that if you are driving, there is very limited parking down at the Marina Piccola. So best is to take a taxi. Parking will cost you about 20 Euros for the day.

TIP> If you would like to "do" the Amalfi drive (which makes the Pacific Coast Highway look like a straight line) there are three ways:

TIP> Take the blue bus:

Just in front of the Sorrento Circumvisuviana rail station there are small blue buses. These buses go down the Amalfi coast making stops at major points. They are quite in-expensive. All of them will stop in Positano, where you can get off, shop, go to the beach and have a nice lunch. Afterwards catch the bus in the opposite direction. It will be marked Sorrento. The nice thing about the blue bus is that it's only about $5 one way to the end of the line in Amalfi. You can also purchase a combo ticket that allows on and off and a return all day. Tickets are sold in the Sorrento rail station. Suggest you check the schedule a day before and arrive early to get a seat on the right-hand side (not the driver side) for the best view of the coast. On the return you want a seat on the driver side.

You Need to Know Before You Go

TIP> Hire a private driver for the day: This is the least stressful and the most enjoyable.

You will notice at many of the travel agents in Sorrento signs stating "all day Amalfi Drive via private car". I have always found these rates rather steep until I found Sorrentocars.com (also known as Leonardotravels.com). Please check out their website and email "Ugo" the owner for the best rate. Make sure you tell him that you read about Sorrentocars in one of Bob Kaufman's books on Italy.

You can't beat this day trip; absolutely no stress, no parking worries and no accidents! The price even gets better if you can get another couple to join you. My suggestion is to have your driver pick you up about 10AM and return you about 5PM and do have the driver arrange lunch for you just outside of Ravello. After lunch visit the villa and gardens of "Ruffalo" just off the main square in Ravello. About 4PM head back to Sorrento.

TIP> Or Drive it yourself:

This is very stressful but very "macho" if you are a guy. Hopefully you have a very good marriage or it may even cause a divorce (just kidding). The second problem you are up against is parking. There is a paid parking garage just inside Positano, however, forget parking on the street. You can't really navigate off the main street of Positano unless you are a billygoat. Secondly, you will not be able to enjoy the views if you are concentrating on the road, or at least what's coming in the opposite direction. You are lucky in one respect in that full size tour buses are prohibited from driving the Amalfi coast.

TIP> If you are driving, suggest you do not attempt to drive further then the town of Amalfi.

It will take you much longer to go back to Sorrento via Salerno. I have done it and you can trust me on this one.   Best is to reverse direction at Amalfi and head back to Sorrento.

ITALY Over 300 Critical Tips

TIP> Before you attempt to do the Amalfi drive consult the Google maps: Sorrento to Amalfi and check out those hairpins turns and switchbacks. If you don't have a headache when you arrive in Amalfi, you will certainly have one when you return to your hotel in Sorrento.

TIP> If you are doing the Amalfi Drive yourself in the winter months when the sun goes about 5PM make sure you reverse direction and give yourself enough time to return to Sorrento during the light hours. There are minimal or no lights on the drive.

You Need to Know Before You Go

---- ITINERARY EXTENSION ----
MILAN AND THE LAKES
AFTER VENICE

TIP> You can visit three of the most beautiful of the Italian Lakes: Como, Maggiore, and Lugano along with Milan after you conclude your visit to Venice. You will need an extra two or three days. Here is how you do it:
Instead of going to Venice's Marco Polo airport on Day 10 for your flight home, you board a train right after breakfast to Milan from either Venice or Venice Mestre. You will base yourself at a hotel within a 10 minute walk to the Milano Centrale rail station. From here you will take day trips to Lake Como, Lugano and Maggiore.

On a side note, I was never turned on by Lugano even though it has a nice shopping area. The problem is that while the lake is half in Italy and half in Switzerland the town of Lugano is in Switzerland where prices are out of sight if you are arriving from Italy! Please see my paragraph below describing why the prices are out of sight. The second problem is that the price of a round trip rail ticket from Milan exceeds $100 because it is a European intercity fare. Take a look at my suggested itinerary:

On Day 10 Train (or you can drive) Venice to Milan
 Afternoon visit to the Cathedral and Galleria Vittorio Emanuele
Day 11 day trip to Lake Como, Bellagio and Varenna
Day 12 day trip Lake Maggiore-Stresa, the Borromean Islands
Day 13 day trip to Lugano or fly home from Milan if you care not to visit Lugano, Switzerland.

Here is the scoop about Switzerland and Lugano. Switzerland has always been an "odd ball" country. Even today they are part of the European union, however they pick and choose which benefits they want. Like the United Kingdom they are on their own currency, the Swiss Franc. However, their cost of living and their standard of living are dramatically different than the other countries in Europe, especially Italy. I just think it's a big joke. Let me explain using American Dollars. A Big Mac at McDonalds is $12. Not a problem if you are working behind the counter. That person prepping your Big Mac doesn't get $25,000 per year she gets $50,000 per year. Everything costs double. But the wages are double. This only affects travelers visiting Switzerland that are use to paying $6 for a Big Mac (at least in Italy); so, in terms of shopping, no big deals here. Everything will cost about double except if you live and work in Switzerland.

TIP> It is best to take day trips out of Milan to the "Lakes" using rail, instead of using a rental car. You can certainly drive from Venice to Milan, however on arrival in Milan it is best to turn in your rental. There are numerous rental car offices in and around the Milano Centrale train station. You must plan this when you rent your car. Using rail will eliminate stress and minimize travel time from Milan thus maximizing the amount of time you have for sightseeing. It is also difficult to find parking in Stresa on Lake Maggiore or Bellagio and Varenna on Lake Como.

TIP> You may want to arrange your days in Milan to take in the massive street market "Mercato Rionale". It is located a few blocks from the Milano Centrale rail station. It's held on Tuesday and Saturday.
If you are lucky to arrive in Milan on either one of these days you can take in the street market and the Cathedral and save the other days for the lakes. If you are taking the train from Milan or driving, you need to depart by 8-9AM since the street market closes about 2-3PM.

You Need to Know Before You Go

TIP> if you are not "shopped out" at the street market you will find the major shopping district of Milan about two blocks away (it runs parallel to the street market) and is known as the Corso Buenos Aires. Here you will find shops for about every price and lots of places to have lunch or enjoy a café and a great Italian pastry; diet when you get back.

TIP> On Day 11 leave after breakfast for your day trip to Lake Como. You do not want to go to the City of Como. It's on a different rail line. You want to take the train to the station known as Varenna-Esino. It's on the line which ends in Tirano which is at the base of the Alps.

Trains leave every hour from Milano Centrale and the round trip cost is about $25. And do purchase a round trip ticket since sometimes the ticket office is closed. You will pay an extra Euro on the train. You can also buy a return ticket on your arrival at Varenna-Esino.

TIP> Always ask if there is a senior rate. Many times there is, and you will be afforded a discounted rate. This is usually true for the Trenitalia division known as Trennord, which operates the trains across the Piedmont and Lombardy regions of northern Italy.

TIP> At Milano Centrale all the rest rooms are on the lower level. Trains depart on the uppermost level, of the three levels. You will need a one Euro coin to enter the ultra-clean facilities. Also note that all Trennord trains have on-board modern restroom facilities.

Seats are un-reserved and the price is the same for any train. The ride is only one hour. On train arrival follow the crowd down the path or the steps to the dock at Varenna. It is best to walk into town and grab a lunch or else buy your ferry ticket (about 6 Euros) to Bellagio. It's only a 10 minute ride to the middle of Lake Como where you will find Bellagio at the top of the peninsular jutting into the lake. There are also lots of restaurants and cafes. So if you did not get enough nourishment in Varenna, consider having lunch in Bellagio.

TIP> On arrival at Bellagio there is a 30 minute tram tour of the town, the mansions and estates. And get this, it's only 5 Euros a person, what a deal. If you arrive at the tram departure point, right opposite the ferry terminal and don't see the tram, don't worry it will be back in a few minutes. After the tram tour enjoy your lunch, shop and down a gelato for a snack.

TIP> If you haven't visited Varenna, purchase a ticket in Bellagio to go there. Note, do not accidently take the wrong ferry and wind up in Cadenabbia. If you do, you will have to get a ferry back to Bellagio then on to Varenna.

TIP> On arrival at the ferry terminal in Varenna, there is a rather difficult "hike" back to the train station. If you are short on time or think you might be short on breath, best is to take a taxi right from the ferry terminal. It will cost you no more than five Euros. The taxis are located to your left of the ferry terminal, directly in front of the colorful Hotel Olivedo.

TIP> Once you arrive via taxi in five minutes at the train station or walk uphill in about 15 minutes, you need to validate your return train ticket in the machine. Consult the chapter on Rail Travel.

TIP> On arrival back at Milano Centrale you will find some excellent and inexpensive restaurants to

You Need to Know Before You Go

your left as you exit the main entrance to the station.

TIP> On Day 12 my suggestion is to visit beautiful Lake Maggiore and the town of Stresa. This is an easy rail trip, but to do it in your rental car will take about 90 minutes at a minimum to get out to Stresa and extreme difficulty finding parking. So after breakfast go over to Milano Centrale and purchase roundtrip tickets to Stresa. Roundtrip tickets cost about ten dollars and the trip takes about an hour with no stress.

Lake Maggiore is known for two things: The famous Borromean Islands which are located about one half mile off the shore of Stresa and the Lake itself. I say the Lake itself because like Lugano and Como, it was also formed by the last ice age and has beautiful mountains abutting it. Off in the distance you can see Switzerland. Now here is the important part. Would you believe Lake Maggiore was the final chapter in Ernest Hemingway's *"A Farewell to Arms"*. Let me explain.

If you read the book or just happened to see the movie (still available on Amazon's movie library) the final chapter in this World War One drama, is where Ernest Hemingway (Frederic Henry) rows across the Lake with his pregnant girl friend, Catherine to neutral Switzerland to escape the Italian army. If he is captured by the Italian army, he will be considered AWOL and a deserter, and probably will be shot. What's more interesting is that the journey takes place in the middle of a stormy night. And yes, he and Catherine do make it to neutral Switzerland (end of story). When you get to Stresa and Lake Maggiore take a look at the Lake and vision Ernest Hemingway rowing across it. Okay, so much for Hemingway; now onto the Borromean Islands.

Two of the islands are worth visiting as the third island (Isola Madre) is a bird sanctuary. Of the two remaining islands Isola

ITALY Over 300 Critical Tips

Bella is my favorite. It is home to the Borromean Palace and gardens (Palazzo Borromeo). There is a separate admission to take a tour of the palace and well worth it. The other island is the Superiore-Pescatori with lots of shops and restaurants.

TIP> On arrival at the Stresa rail station, it's only a short walk to the ferry terminal (traghetti). Just follow the crowd. On arrival at the ferry terminal best is to purchase the combo ticket to the Isola Bella and Superiore-Pescatore
From the Stresa ferry terminal to any of the islands it's only 15 minutes and from island to island it's also 15 minutes. Ferries run about every 30 minutes. And yes, the ferry company takes all credit cards and has senior rates. Also note, do not get a ferry accidently back to Baveno. You need to go back to Stresa.

TIP> The island of Isola Bella and Superiore-Pescatore are rather small and there are well maintained walkways which will allow you to walk completely around each island. The walk is no more than a half mile.

TIP> My suggestion is to visit the island of Isola Bella first and take the tour of the Palazzo Borromeo before having lunch. Then have lunch on Isola Bella or continue to the second island, Superiore-Pescatore for lunch and more shopping.
About 5 or 6PM take the ferry back to Stresa (not Baveno, it's on a different rail line) and make your way back to the Stresa rail station. If you are too "pooped" from all that walking a taxi will take you to the rail station for five Euros.

TIP> Consider having lunch at either island, there are plenty of places. Best locations are cafes with a view of the mountains of Switzerland.

You Need to Know Before You Go

TIP> If you are concluding your visit to Italy in Milan you need to know that there are two major airports. Most flights to the USA depart from MXP (Malpensa). Many flights requiring connections in Europe depart via Linate Airport (LIN). Make sure you know which airport you are flying out of.

Now on to Lugano and Lake Lugano:

TIP> If you do go to Lugano for the day, don't worry about converting to Swiss Francs. Most of the merchants will take your Euros at a favorable exchange rate. However, if purchasing anything, best is to use your credit card and get the rock-bottom bank rate.

TIP> If you have carry-on bags (rollies) for your trip to Italy, consider flying home from Zurich. You will need to take your rollies with you and drag them around Lugano before you head to Zurich.

TIP> Enjoy lunch in Lugano. You should note that the rail station is located on a hill overlooking the city. Follow the crowd and down the escalators to the city.

TIP> Instead of Lugano, Switzerland, consider going to Zurich, Switzerland (and ending your visit to Italy) via the Bernina Express. Special trains operated by the RhB railway go over the Alps from the Italian town of Tirano to the Swiss town of Chur. From Chur you can take the 90 minute train to Zurich. You can visit the Bernina Express website at Rhb.com. It is best to overnight in Zurich before flying home the next day.

You can find out more in my book "*Italy The Best Places to See by Rail*" where I have devoted an entire chapter on how to do this. The Bernina Express is up there with the Orient Express and the Glacier Express. It's only a four hour trip on a special train but the scenery is jaw-dropping.

TIP> You can't visit Lugano and then go to Zurich via the Bernina Express since they are on different rail lines. If you want to go to Zurich via Lugano, you can, but you will go under the Alps via the Gotthard tunnels on the high speed Euro trains as opposed to over the Alps on the Bernina Express.

CHAPTER 3

HOTELS & RESERVATIONS

INTRODUCTION-

The hotel or lodging industry in Italy is quite complex to say the least. Italy as the most visited country in Western Europe has its share of all types of hotels, B&B's, villas, castles, palaces and you name it.

Throughout this book I will refer to the generic name of a hotel which may also take the form of a B&B, Residenza d Epoca, villa, pensione, albergo or what have you.

For the same price as a regular hotel you can stay at one of these "alternate type" hotels. You will also find them in major cities and not just in the countryside.

If you want a good book on staying at these villas, castles, palaces, etc. consult my book *ITALY Skip the Hotel and Stay at a Palace, For the Same Price Live Like a King.* You can find it on Amazon.com or at Barnes and Nobles or your favorite bookshop can order it.

Only true or what we would call "classic" hotels are rated by the Federal Government. They range from one star to five star. A superior rating can also boost them higher i.e. four and five star superior.

Bed and Breakfasts and other places of stays i.e. Albergos, Residenza d' Epoca's (which are converted old buildings that are now hotels) and Agriturismos are usually not rated.

ITALY Over 300 Critical Tips

Here is my description of each category:

Hotels are 10-300 rooms and usually offer private baths. Most hotels, even one star (see below) offer a breakfast even if it is a cup of coffee and a hard roll. As most of us are familiar with hotels, I won't dwell anymore on this.

On the lower end of the spectrum are the pensiones. It's the word pension with an "e" on the end. They are basically like a hostel or a YMCA. These sleeping establishments cater to the real budget minded. Rooms come in one or two beds and usually have a sink. However, you may have to use a shared bath (toilet and shower) down the hallway. When you book a pensione you should make sure you have a private full bath and not just a sink (if that's what you want). Many of them because of numerous B&B's offer a breakfast of coffee and a roll. Rooms are extremely limited. They can also be booked on most of the booking engines. Don't expect a great mattress on a box spring. Most have a mattress on a steel bed with springs. Depending on where you are in Italy rates are usually less than $50 for a room for two.

Bed and Breakfasts (B&B's): There is nothing wrong with a bed and breakfast establishment. I am not talking about an AirBnB where someone gives you a bedroom in their apartment or home for the night. The true B&B's usually have less than ten rooms and of course breakfast is usually included. On the breakfast there will be in addition to coffee and teas, sweet rolls, cereals and other cold items. Many times hot dishes will be offered. Two things you should know about B&B's: The walls and doors tend to be paper thin and sometimes all the guests must eat breakfast together i.e. breakfast is served at 8AM. You need to check for basics i.e. air-conditioning, WIFI, etc. Of major concern is allergies to dogs and cats if the B&B allows them. It is best to check via email before booking.

Albergos: Many times you will see a small hotel with a green little sign and the word "Albergo". I won't go into the history

You Need to Know Before You Go

of the name but suffice it to say it's usually a two or three star small hotel.

Residenza d' Epoca's, Villas, Palazzos, Castles, etc. are usually converted buildings which according to the government must be at least 100 years old. These are extremely unique types of establishments to stay in and quite an experience. This past September (2019) en route to Alborobello (the home of the Trulli houses), we stayed at the Castel Limatola. I might note that yes, you could play football in the room and yes it was a room out of Versailles. What an enjoyable experience.

Another very popular lodging establishment is the Agriturismo. Basically, it is identical to a Bed and Breakfast, except it is a real farm. The farm usually grows their own fruits and vegetables and may have livestock. What I like best about the Agriturismo is that practically everything comes from the farm, including fresh eggs for breakfast. Because they grow as much as they can you will find many Agriturismos offer dinner as an option. You should check if during your stay this will be possible. Sometimes they only offer dinner on the weekends, sometimes only during the season. It is best to ask in an email.

You should consider making your visit to Italy a more enjoyable experience by staying at these unique establishments. Best to pick-up a copy of my book at Amazon.com.

Now if you are staying at a hotel and it is government rated here is a description of what to expect:

One Star Hotels- Defines the words "You get what you pay for". These hotels border on a hostel, a dorm room or just staying at the YMCA. In Italy many of them are called Pensions. Many have shared baths i.e. it's up the hallway about 50 feet. I am sure you know what I mean. If they have linoleum tile, or indoor outdoor carpeting, you are in a one star hotel. Usually there is no breakfast or just a coffee, roll with butter and jam. Expect to pay $40-$50 per night. You won't find many or any at all on the booking engines. However, if you do an organic search you may find it on page 45. Another way to spot them is to use Google Maps. Just enlarge the map around the area you wish to stay and they will pop up.

Two Star Hotels- They are a cut above the one star hotel. Most have private baths. Breakfast is one of those "hi-carb" breakfasts of cereal, toast and coffee and that's it. Don't ask for scrambled eggs or a basket of assorted sweet-rolls. Expect to pay $50-$80 per night. Once again consult Google Maps and then look further for a website.

Three Star Hotels- There is a marked difference between three star hotels and two star hotels. Three star hotels are basically the same as American chain type hotels, only with the exception of the low end budget type. They are best compared to the American (and Canadian) type hotels which offer a hot breakfast of make your own waffles, some type of protein i.e. eggs, yogurt, several type of juices, etc. They may even have a restaurant which will be open for dinner. Room service may be available. These rooms will cost you $80-$150 per night.

Four star hotels- They will have the same amenities of the three star hotels but will also have usually four additional major features. One will be a concierge desk to help you out with sightseeing tours, recommendations on restaurants, etc. They will also have a lobby bar and most of them will have at least one restaurant which is open for dinner. In addition, they will definitely have room service. A four star hotel may be also classified as a Four Star Superior. What this means is that they will have other amenities, such as a spa which will offer massages, facials, etc., most of us know these as "resorts". Expect to pay $100-160 per night for a room.

Five star hotels- These hotels are in a class usually reserved for the "A" list people. They may be historic and are truly elegant.

You Need to Know Before You Go

If you are driving, they will not have parking lots but valets. Because they are five star and define the word "pricey", they do not include breakfast, that would be too common. Instead they will offer breakfast for a fee which may run from 20 Euros a person on up. The breakfast is usually a lavish buffet complete with an omelet station. If you care not to partake in the buffet, of course you can order off the menu. Expect to pay 4-5 Euros for a bottomless cup of coffee.

Believe it or not, there is also a class of a five star superior. Expect these hotels which are often resorts to offer everything you could imagine. And yes, if you put your shoes outside the door at night they will shine them. And, do make sure you pull up in your luxury car driven by your Italian driver. No small car rentals here. Because five star hotels are in a class by themselves expect to pay $250-2,000 per night.

There is no rhyme or reason on how the government classifies hotels. What I mean is that there are no hard rules. Yes, one star and two star, no problem. You would probably rate them like I would rate them and the government would also. However, when it comes to three and four star hotels, it becomes a little more difficult.

Just like one star hotels, the same is true for five star hotels. You will know it when you walk in the lobby that you are in a five star hotel. The problem is between the three and four star hotels. Let me explain.

I have stayed in many four star hotels which I would have classified as a three star hotel. Likewise, I have stayed at many three star hotels which should have been classified as four star hotels.

ITALY Over 300 Critical Tips

---------- HOTEL SELECTION ----------

TIP> If you are going to Italy, try to stay at European style hotels i.e. small elevators, cozy rooms, etc. Avoid US style mega hotels where you can use your hotel points. You can stay at these hotels anytime. You are here to experience Italy.

TIP> Many large American type chains have their hotels near the airport or on the outskirts of major cities, mostly Rome.

I know someone who used their hotel "points" only to find out they had to take a taxi in and out of Rome each day. It cost them $90 per day. Better would be to stay in the heart of Rome.

TIP> Sometimes the difference between a four star hotel and a three star hotel may be only a few dollars. Sometimes they may be the same price. So, what goes? Best is then to read the reviews and use my scoring TIP below.

TIP> Before selecting any hotel make yourself a checklist of exactly what amenities you must unconditionally have.

I don't know how many times I have heard "I booked this great three star hotel in the hills of Chianti only to find out they did not have air-conditioning. I enquired at the front desk to find out, "you don't need A/C in the evenings in Chianti they are always cool, that's why we don't have it". Okay. That's an acceptable answer. However, I can't sleep without A/C even if it's Italy. I should have asked; my error.

Here is a suggested checklist to eliminate any surprises, stress and a potential divorce. Make a list of them, and then make copies with the name of the hotel on the top. They are in somewhat importance:

You Need to Know Before You Go

Free Parking- on premises or elsewhere, do you have to pay? Bear in mind that some hotels may be as much as 30 Euros per night to park your chariot plus that valet tip.

Free WIFI – Yes, some establishments still charge for it.

Air Conditioning- Heating in the off-season or winter months?

Elevator – If more than two stories. Most of the time there will be someone to help you with your bags. However, you may have to walk up those stairs several times a day. Ask for a ground floor room (Ground floor is the Zero floor). Do not use the term first floor. It is not the ground floor. The first floor is above the ground floor (Zero Floor).

Breakfast included- what type? Read the reviews on this one.

Other wants if important- Is there a fridge in the room for your medications, baby's food, or leftovers, if you will be staying several days. And finally…

Location- As Baron Hilton said, location, location, location. If you have to add a taxi ride each way of $25 you probably could have stayed at a more expensive "closer in" hotel.

TIP> If you are concerned with the size of the room because you will be living out of it for three or more days, you should consider the size. If it is not stated in the booking engine's website e.g. booking.com or whatever booking engine you prefer, best is to email the hotel directly and ask what is the size of the room in square meters? Here are your answers:

Less than 20 square meters (180 sq. feet) - It's a little tight.

About 30 square meters (270 sq. feet) Room is just okay.

About 40 square meters (about 360 sq. feet)- It's the size of the standard American hotel chain room (10 feet by 40 feet)

Over 50 square meters (450-700 sq. feet) - Best to bring a football or a nerf ball in your suitcase.

If you want to make a quick comparison of room size, remember that real small room in Paris where you had to put your bags on top of each other and get out of the bed on only one side because your bags were on the other. Yup, that room was ten feet by ten feet (100 sq. feet) or about 11 square meters or about 99 square feet (close enough). You had to sleep with the windows open just to get enough oxygen.

TIP> When looking at the listings on booking engines, you should note the small diagrams of the beds. They have something in Italy which they do not have in America or in Canada. No, I am not talking about the bidet in the bathroom, does anyone ever use this? It's not a King, Queen or even a Single bed. It's a picture of two single beds pushed together. There will usually be a "vane" in the middle. The beds can be easily pushed apart to create two single beds giving the establishment more options to sell the room. It you definitely want a "true" king and don't want that vane in the middle, you must specify a MATRIMONIAL bed. Obviously this is best for those couples who are on a honeymoon.

TIP> You should use the reviews as a final selection, by using this technique which I call the Satisfaction Experience.
Use Booking.com or Tripadvisor.com. Take the total number of reviews. Use this as the denominator and then place the total of the bottom two categories (either poor and very poor or terrible and poor) as the numerator. If the percent is say 20% or more, you may not want to stay there, since one out of five did not like it and gave it a rather negative rating.

Here is an example: 4780 reviews, 1160 fell into the bottom two categories of reviews. The "The Satisfaction Experience" would be 1160/4780 times 100 or 24%. As for me, I would not stay there.

You Need to Know Before You Go

TIP> When reading reviews, you should take a look at the bottom two categories for the most recent reviews. Don't look at reviews of several years ago. The establishment may have corrected the WIFI or the A/C problem or in fact may have completely renovated the property.

Here are some recent negative reviews on a property:

"We were in Rome in May and the A/C in our room did not cool it down, they switched our room and the same problem". There were other comments about the fact that the fan in the A/C unit rattled and it kept us up all night.

"The WIFI only worked within 30 feet of the front desk. We could not use it in our room; many comments like this".

Comments like the above may put the "kabash" on the hotel under consideration. Next.

TIP> Absolutely disregard ridiculous comments like "The front desk manager was grumpy" and "my martini at the lobby bar was warm."

TIP> I have read what I believe is the most popular of the negative reviews as "the hotel was too far away from where all the sites were". Well duh... did you spot it on the map?

In general the rates usually go down depending on how far you are from the center of the town or the Historic District (Centro Storico). A four star hotel in Rome known as the Grand Hotel Fleming in a lovely residential neighborhood is a little over $100 per night and the rooms are quite large. It's located on a little square where there is an open market each morning. You can reach the Rome Metro by bus in 15 minutes. There is a taxi stand across from the hotel where you can pile four people in a car for 20-25 Euros and be in the Historic District in 15 minutes. There are lots of local restaurants in the neighborhood, ATM's, grocery stores, dry cleaners, etc.

Now compare the above with a four star hotel within a few blocks of the Historic District. It will cost you about 400-500 Euros per night and you will have to deal with all the noise of the motorcycles and the traffic. Welcome to Rome!

So, do read the reviews.

TIP> Most establishments impose a mandated tax by the municipality of 3-6 Euros per night per room. This is not a "shakedown". The amount you will pay depends on the star rating of the hotel. The more stars the greater the tax. Here is the problem... You must pay this in cash, no credit cards. Don't think the hotel is pulling a fast one. This is the norm in Italy... cash for the local tax.

TIP> If you are travelling as a single, you will find that you will be penalized for a double room.
What I mean by this is that a three star hotel room for two may cost you say 100 Euros. However, if one person occupies it you will pay the single supplement. So, it's not 50 Euros, it's 50 Euros plus the single supplement of 25 Euros for a total of 75 Euros. That's exactly what they call it, The Single Supplement. Best is to ask if they have single room rates.

TIP> Use the travel search engines i.e. Orbitz, Expedia, etc. to see if you can obtain the best rate. Frankly, I prefer Booking.com.
I find with Booking.com I can cancel a reservation easily. Each confirmation is printed with a booking code and a pin on it. It's just easier to manage and there is no need to sign in with passwords and all that other stuff.

You Need to Know Before You Go

TIP> Don't be fooled by "portal web sites" that claim they have the lowest rates. They don't! The hotel has only one rate for the type of room you want. Sure, if you compare rates across several websites you may find a lesser rate. However, that lesser rate may have severe restrictions on it. So, if it's less money, it's probably a non-refundable rate. Or, you get no breakfast. No free beer here!

TIP> Don't be fooled when you see on a booking engine the words "Sold Out" or "Sold out on our site". If you contact the hotel directly they will probably have rooms at a good rate.
The reason the booking engine says "Sold Out" is because the hotel may pull the dates because they know they will statistically sell out all the rooms for that night. So why would they want to part with a 20% commission to the booking engine when there is no need to. Many hotels will pull the dates off the booking engine when they get to 75% booked.

TIP> When viewing booking engines and hotel websites you may not see certain dates listed in the future. What I mean is that those dates have not opened up yet. A short email to the hotel is best to obtain a short reply "We will open up those dates for the summer of 2021 in February".

TIP> If you can't locate the hotel's official website, you can email them easily. Well over 90% of all hotels in Italy use the following format: info@*thehotelyyouwant*.com or .it (dot it).

TIP> After you research the hotel (or whatever) you wish to stay at, you should see if you can make a direct booking. Many times, different types of rooms are available and sometimes discounts are given for a senior rate, multiple room nights and more. You will not see this on the booking engines. In addition, many times with a direct booking you will receive a free gift. Perhaps it will be a free bottle of wine or something else.

TIP> Avoid committing for the Non-Refundable rate if you are using a booking engine. It is definitely not worth the risk unless you are in Italy and you will be checking into that hotel in a few days.
Also, if you make a mistake i.e. on the check-in date, you will "own" the room. However, if you booked directly with a small hotel, they will always want to accommodate you. Opps, "I made a mistake and wanted to check in on October 10th, instead of the 11th." Not a problem. You won't be able to do this at all with any type of non-refundable rate via a booking engine, trust me on this one.

TIP> When reserving a room either through a booking engine or directly with the hotel, it is best to ask for a quiet room.
Many of the hotels in large cities (obviously not in the Tuscan Countryside) are on major boulevards where you can hear lots of noise all day and even at night. Motorcycles and scooters also add to the noise. Do ask for a QUIET room. Many of these will be facing a courtyard or a side street. On check in note the noise level. If it's not acceptable ask the front desk for another room, before you move your bags from the lobby into the room. It's best to arrange this on your booking. In this way the room can be set aside for you and will be held for your arrival.

TIP> Many smaller hotels do not list on all booking engines or any booking engines at all. I use Google Maps to spot hotels and then Google their name or send an email directly to them using the format I stated above. It works all the time.
Okay so much for booking. Now, on to checking in.

You Need to Know Before You Go

----- CHECKING INTO YOUR HOTEL -----

TIP> You should email all the hotels and confirm your days of arrival. Also in the same email do ask them how late you can check in. Many B&B's may close the front door at 10PM or so. You may be out of luck if you arrive at 1AM and are forced to check into a four or five star hotel a few blocks away. And by the way, don't even consider asking the B&B to refund your one night because you did not make it there in time. Remember, it was held in your name for the night; just chalk it up to experience.

It may be better to call ahead or at least have a stand-up bar or that gelato shop make the call and explain the problem. Hopefully, they will stay open for your arrival or perhaps leave the front key and your room key with the bar down the street.

TIP> You should check into your hotel in daylight and give yourself an hour of "get lost time". If sunset is 5PM, it would be best to arrive 3-4PM.

What you don't want to do is arrive at your hotel after the sun has gone down. It is a major hassle. Sometimes for us macho guys it can even cause a divorce!

Finding your hotel in major cities in the dark may be a problem. I drove around one town (Chivari) in Italy for at least a half hour before someone who knew, told me exactly how to get to the hotel. And yes, I was using my GPS, no help!

The problem is further compounded when you are trying to locate your hotel in the countryside, perhaps in Greve-in-Chianti. You will find the signs really small and there won't be many of them. And let's face it, how many people will you find on those local roads where you can do a "shout-out" and ask directions, especially at 9PM. And, if it's raining it gets worse. Like who is walking around the vineyards or picking olives in the rain? It is further complicated by the fact that most of the locals don't speak much English. Best to always have a pencil and paper where you can scribble the hotels name on, else use the "Dough vey..... name of hotel". They will motion with their hands (as most Italians do). Just make sure you remember those hand gestures.

TIP> It may be difficult to check into many hotels located either in a ZTL or on a hill top.
Remember in one of my earlier chapters that a ZTL (Zone Traffic Limited) is a street you are not allowed in unless you have a pass by the Police Department. Once you land in it (like Monopoly) and a police officer observes you, you need to get assistance from the front desk of the hotel, else a stiff fine.

Best is to email the hotel and ask them what to do. Many will say, "park in the square and have the gelato store call us and we will come down with a pass for the ZTL".

TIP> You should read up on the hotel before you leave home. Many hotels are in the historic district (Centro Storico) or may be on small alleys or on hills which are difficult to navigate, even with a small car. I found this true in Sorrento and the hilltop town of Erice in Sicily.
As stated before, best to have the local stand-up bar or the gelato shop call the hotel. Many times they will send down a bellmen or a porter to bring your bags up to the hotel. They will then tell you where to park your car. Make sure you give the helper a few Euros for his effort.

TIP> While Italy is quite safe, when you move that car to the municipal parking area (a garage or a lot), make sure you put that GPS and your camera in the glove compartment and double check that the windows are raised tight and the car is locked and further don't leave anything on the seats.

You Need to Know Before You Go

TIP> On arrival at your hotel in Italy the front desk person may take your passports. They usually make copies of them and may submit nightly reports on-line to the local police department. Just make sure they give them back when you leave.
On a side note, unlike the USA and Canada, they will not request a credit card up-front. You are on the honor system and will be expected to pay with cash or a credit/debit card on departure. Remember, many do not take American Express.

TIP> Is it double dipping (into your pocket) or double tipping? Most four and five star (definitely) hotels have doormen who help you bring your bags into the lobby. After you check-in and are satisfied with your hotel room (see below) a bellmen is called to assist you with bringing your bags to your room. You need to tip them both.
Oh, also you need to tip the valet who will stash your chariot. I make it a habit of only tipping the valet when the car is returned to me. Remember also that most of these "helpers" earn their money through tips. You should consider a minimum of two Euros for the doorman and the bellman unless you have a boat load of bags.

TIP> On arrival make sure you check the rate you are being charged and the day you are expected to checkout. No surprises here!

TIP> After checking into a hotel do not take your baggage to the room. Instead check out the room first. Leave your bags with the exception of your carryon's (and lady's handbag) and find the room first and check it out. Hopefully, the bellman will first show you the room.
First thing you need to do is put the air-conditioner on. While the room is getting cold (hopefully), put the TV on and make

sure it is operational. Take a look at the bathroom and make sure it is up to par.

If you requested a quiet room, make sure it is not facing a major boulevard, not next to the elevator and not next to the soda or ice machine, if they have one. The worst thing you want to hear is ice cubes or cans of soda dropping all night. These machines are rare in European hotels, but you never know.

TIP> If you are just arriving from an overnight flight from the USA or Canada make sure the room can be darkened to your liking.

TIP> After you inspect the room and find it too small, ask the front desk clerk.. "is it possible to have a larger (grande) room"?
Don't say anything about price. Let him give you the key so you can inspect the larger room. Do the same you did with the smaller room i.e. test the A/C, turn on the TV and see if the room is quiet. If you like it, report back to the front desk person and say "that larger room would be great". If he says it will cost you 10 Euros more and you feel it is worth it then go for it. If he says "no problem, you can have it, same price" you just lucked out. When you are happy with the room, then request the bellmen to help you with your bags and do tip him.

TIP> If you are driving and the hotel has a garage, you should be advised that many of the garages are quite small and difficult to maneuver in. After parking the car in the check-in area, I usually take a look at the garage and observe the "scrapes" on the side of those concrete columns. If I find that it is too tight for me, I have the bellmen or the valet stash my chariot. In this way I don't have the stress and further a scrape on the side of the car when I return it to the rental car company.

66

You Need to Know Before You Go

TIP> After breakfast, do leave a few coins or even a Euro on the table for the person who pours the coffee or removes the plates.

TIP> If you have been leaving those coins on the table after breakfast you should not have any problem asking the wait person to put those "mushy and wet scrambled eggs" in the microwave or a fry pan and cook them well.

Most Americans and in fact Canadians, don't eat runny, mushy scrambled eggs. Don't know what it is with the Italians. I know one thing...they don't eat American hot breakfasts.

TIP> If you are bothered by that fan in the bathroom which always turns on with the light, consider a 220volt night light.

TIP> Also consider carrying in your bag a 220volt emersion heater. It is excellent to make a cup of tea in the evening when you are at a B&B or an agriturismo. I carry tea bags and coffee "soluble" packets with me so I can make a hot drink any time. If you need a tea cup just ask the front desk.

You can usually pickup a 220volt night light and an immersion heater at any hardware store in Italy. Just ask the front desk person or anyone, even in a small town for the *"Ferramenta"* or better "dov'è il negozio di ferramenta?"

TIP> If you have one of those hotel keys tied onto a bowling ball or something similar, you must turn it in each time you exit the hotel. Do not leave it on the upper counter of the check in desk such that anyone can lift it off. Drop it in front of the desk clerk or ask him/her to put it away please.

ITALY Over 300 Critical Tips

TIP> If you are staying at a B&B, Agriturismo, or a pensione, etc., do make sure you know how to operate the lock on the front door.
It will be difficult to call anyone at midnight when you are locked out. Best also to get an emergency telephone number.

TIP> If you are staying at an agriturismo in the country side, and you will be going out for dinner, do check Google Maps for the local eateries which will be serving dinner. Also remember how to get back to your agriturismo in the dark. If you do not want to go out for dinner, and instead wish to "bring-in" (Brits call it Take-Away) you can usually request utensils from the proprietor on your return from your day of sightseeing. They will be glad to help you out and will welcome the pleasure to provide this service. Enjoy your wine, cheese, salumi, olives and that crusty bread.

TIP> You can avoid those in-room mini-bar outrageous charges by buying your bottled water and those cans of Coke at a local "Alimentaria". You will find they will be a fraction of the price. And, don't forget the almonds and the potato chips also available at the local alimentaria.

TIP> It is best to purchase one of those multi-function knifes (like a Swiss Army knife) with even a corkscrew if you enjoy wine and keep it with your tooth brush. In this way you will be able to cut cheese and salumi (salami) in your room for a picnic on that country road in Tuscany.
Remember you cannot pack this item in your handbag or your carry on since it will be confiscated by the TSA people.

# # #

CHAPTER 4

DRIVING IN ITALY

TIP> It's really a rule. Never, never, never, drive in Rome. Not Italy, just in Rome.
My suggestion is always take the Leonardo Express, a taxi, or a limo from Rome's Fiumicino airport to your hotel in Rome. After visiting Rome go back to the airport and rent your car. Do not under any circumstances rent a car in the city of Rome i.e. near your hotel or where ever and attempt to drive out of the City. This can be a disaster. Repeat again..go back to the airport and rent a car there.

Now, you may ask, "why am I so down in driving in Rome"? There are many reasons. First, Italian drivers are maniacs. Secondly, Rome has lots of ZTL (Zone Traffic Limited) areas. This means if you get caught driving in these areas it will be a stiff fine. Police monitor these areas in person and by cameras. Only certain authorized vehicles can enter these areas i.e. truck deliveries, tour buses, etc. The problem is that once you enter the zone it is difficult to get out of it. It's like one of those mouse traps or better one of those corn mazes. Thirdly, the traffic on many streets in Rome, especially in and around the historic district is unbearable. On one occasion, I was forced to abandon my taxi, pay the charge and walk the additional 10 blocks rather than be stalled in traffic with the taxi meter running. Fourth, Rome has many one way streets and navigating them is nearly impossible and fifth there are very few street lights, you know the ones with the red, green and yellow. I think there may be less than 100.

ITALY Over 300 Critical Tips

One of my friends I gave the above advice told me when he got back that "best advice I learned from Bob about driving in Rome...DON'T". Okay, enough of driving in Rome, just go back to the airport and rent your car there. Enough said.

TIP> When you are renting a car in Italy, don't be fooled by the low price offered e.g. only $6 per day or something so ridiculous. Italy along with Ireland and Israel require mandatory liability insurance. You must look at the total rate offered.

TIP> I suggest always booking the least costly car that will fit your needs. In most situations the rental counter will want to upgrade you to a larger car. Just be firm and state "thanks anyway but I will take the Fiat Panda" or whatever. When you get into the garage the attendant will tell you sometimes, "we are all out of Panda's, so just take any Volkswagen Jetta". Imagine, at the rental counter they were going to upgrade you to a Jetta for only $100 more per week, now you get one at no extra charge.

TIP> Most European cars, especially in the "med" countries are standard transmission. You will pay more for automatics. Remember to book an automatic unit if you cannot drive a standard transmission car.

TIP> Here are my recommendations for renting a car. If you are a solo traveler and have only carry-on luggage you might want to consider the SMART car. It's called the "FOR TWO". It is of course manual transmission, great on the mileage but very uncomfortable for those long Autostrada drives at 70 miles per hour. If you are two people you should consider all models which have four doors and or a

You Need to Know Before You Go

hatchback. If your two bags can't fit in the trunk, it's easy to place one on the back seat if you have four doors. If you have only two doors, it becomes difficult to lift that second bag and place it on the rear seat. Most rental car booking engines i.e. Orbitz, Expedia, etc. show small pictures of how many bags you can put in the car.

TIP> Make sure you bring your GPS with the Italy map loaded on it. And, yes you can also use Google Maps, however, you need to download the route in a WIFI area before you leave your hotel in Rome (or any town in Italy) in order to not be charged for the out-of-sight data roaming charges. So, my tip is just to invest the $100-$150 in a Garmin or Tom Tom unit. And do remember to download the Italy map before you go.

Also remember that gizmo which plugs into the cigarette lighter will work anywhere because it's 12VDC. If you want a USB charger for 220VAC, so you can charge your GPS unit in your hotel room, you can pick one up at any rest stop on the Autostrada. You can also purchase a pack of two at Amazon.com. for about $10. The ID for them is B07GK76GTW.

TIP> If you fly into Rome's FCO (Fiumicino) airport you will find all popular auto rental companies, and also Italian rental companies which you may have not heard about, are located in the parking garage. It is a long walk from Terminals 1, 2 or 3 to the rental counter area located in the main garage. So best is to keep that cart you picked up at no charge at baggage claim, place your bags on it, take the elevator up several levels and follow the signs to the rental counters.

TIP> When you pick up your car make sure the attendant gives you a ticket to exit the parking

71

garage, else you will have to park your rental car and return to the counter for the exit ticket.

TIP> Italy is fussy (like Mexico) about minor damage to rental cars. It is best to do a walk-around with the attendant and note minor scrapes, dings, etc. You may want to take pictures of the car and then snap a picture of the odometer proving the mileage when you left the rental garage. You should check also for missing hubcaps, tools and spare tire in the trunk and broken grills.

TIP> Since Italy is a Mediterranean country and will feel warm even in April-May and September-November, before leaving the rental garage I run my air conditioner and make sure it works. You do not want to get stuck on the way down to Naples only to find the A/C does not work. In addition, make sure the radio works or better bring a CD.

TIP> It is best to check with your credit card company if they have a feature called "Waiver of Deductible". You need not take the collision coverage if you have this feature. If you are involved in an accident your credit card company will pay the first $500 of collision damage and your main auto insurance carrier will pick up the balance. It is best to contact your insurance agent and the credit card company which you will be using for the rental, before leaving the USA.

-------- THE AUTOSTRADA -------- AND OTHER ROADS OF ITALY

Italy has a road system built for tourists and for getting from one location to another location in a short amount of time. It's called the Autostrada. Roads which are part of the system all start with "A", i.e. A1, A13, etc. Pretty much all of the "A" roads are toll. However, access roads like the A91 and loop roads either around major cities e.g. Rome are toll free. Where there are urban areas and where tolls would cause too much traffic delay you will find there is no charge for the Autostrada. Through the Naples and Milan areas you will find no tolls. The same is true on the GRA ring road around Rome. However, once you get out of the urban area, you must pick up a ticket or else have a TELEPASS transponder. If you are going to be in Italy more than two weeks, you may want to consider renting a TELEPASS transponder.

TIP> You should always prefer using the Autostrada between major points as most of the secondary roads are SLOW. This is not a time to be frugal. However, if you take the local roads it will take you twice as long. There is an advantage: you will pass through interesting scenery and small towns affording nice places to enjoy lunch and mingle with the locals. Also, remember you will use more fuel since you can't cruise at 110 kilometers per hour with all those hills, trucks and yes the school buses you will encounter on local roads.

On a personal note, I have taken the E80 coast road from Rome, via Grosetto to Florence two times, and found it most enjoyable. So do consider the secondary "E" roads.

ITALY Over 300 Critical Tips

For every 7 kilometers you travel (not counting the feeder roads like the A91 or the ring roads e.g. the GRA) it will cost you one Euro. So just figure the mileage using Google Maps or whatever and then divide by 7. The cost will usually be a little less. So getting back to how to get out of greater Rome:

So, assuming you took my advice and went back to the airport to rent your car, here is what you need to do to catch the Autostrada north to Tuscany (Firenze), Umbria, etc. or south toward Naples (Napoli), Amalfi, Pompeii, Sorrento, etc.

After exiting the airport follow the signs to Roma. You will be on the A91. In about 8 miles you will see the exit for the GRA also known at the A90 (it's an A road, but there are no tolls). The GRA is the beltway around Rome, just like the Washington Beltway, or the other beltways around our American cities.

The GRA goes totally around the city of Rome. If you go the wrong way you will find you will come back to the airport access road i.e. the A91. If you are going toward Florence you need to follow the signs to Aurelia. Then continue up the GRA till you see the signs to Firenze via the A1. It's a good 26 kilometers or about 20 minutes. If you are going south follow the signs to Napoli and the A1 going south. You don't have to worry, just follow the signs for the cities and it will put you on the A1 either north to Firenze or south to Napoli.

TIP> On entering the toll area of the Autostrada, always stay on your right and pick up a ticket from those "ticket spitters". I will tell you more later about the need to stay on your right when exiting the Autostrada.

TIP> On the Autostradas, the left hand lane i.e. the high speed lane is reserved for the fast cars, or should I say the fast, perhaps what we would call the aggressive drivers. You need to stay in your

You Need to Know Before You Go

right hand lane. Now, if you happen to be in the high speed left hand lane and see no one in your rear-view mirror, don't assume that you have control of that lane. If you take a look in your rear-view mirror, in about a nano-second, you will see another driver on your tail, or should I say on your bumper with his/her left directional blinking. This means "Please get out of my way". It's sought of the rule of the road. You should immediately negotiate into the lane to the right of you, usually the center lane and let that fast driver pass you.

TIP> In Italian *"Controllo elettronico della velocita"* *means electronic speed control or simply,* "Control your Velocity". This is a simple one. It means watch your speed.

When you see this sign it means speed cameras will soon follow. Look for them on the right side of the road usually within a kilometer. They may also use that large oversize structure across the highway to snap a picture of your car. The next one snaps another picture of your car. They compute the number of seconds apart and determine your speed. If it's way over the limit, you guessed it, you get a speeding ticket!

When you get home you will receive a $25 charge from you rental company for doing the research i.e. who drove the car that day. In about 4-6 weeks expect a letter from the government of Italy with a citation for your heavy foot on the metal. You can pay your hefty fine on-line with a credit card.

TIP> If you have any intention on going back to Italy, and hopefully you will, you should pay the fine, else if they pick you up again you will have a lot of explaining to do and you may land in jail. It is best to make a copy of the receipt and stuff it in your passport wallet.

ITALY Over 300 Critical Tips

TIP> Unlike the USA there are rest stops every seven miles on the Autostrada. There are two types. What I call the deluxe type (the Autogrill's and the Sarni's) and the basic ones. Both have gas stations and very clean restrooms. So there is no need to exit the Autostrada to find a half way decent place to have lunch or dinner.

TIP> Before, you order anything at the counter, even a café or an Americano Coffee you must pay for it first at the cashier then show the ticket to the server behind the counter. This eliminates the "the dine and dash" problem. You still pay, same as in America or Canada if the food is served "cafeteria" style and you move and pick and place items on your tray. You simply pay at the cashier at the end of the line. And yes, they will take your plastic cards.

TIP> Be advised that you will have to enter the Autogrill and the Sarni through a turn-style. You must navigate completely through the maze of souvenirs, toys, candy, bags of various types of pasta and gifts before you arrive at the cashier. You can't turn around and go out the same place you entered. The turn-style only goes one way. It's a smart way to have you view everything and perhaps have you do some impulse buying.

TIP> Italians rarely use their horns, only in real emergencies. So suggest you don't either.

TIP> Never insult an Italian (and furthermore no one else) by giving them the finger (the birdie). They may be crazy on the roads but they are gracious and demand respect. It's just their way of driving. You will have to get use to it. Don't take it

You Need to Know Before You Go

personally. In a worse case they will call out to you "hey pasta head next time move over".

TIP> On exiting the Autostrada do not get in any lane with that yellow sign saying "TELEPASS" . Like the USA it's for cars, trucks and buses with TELEPASS transponders. You need to be in the far right line with the big blue signs for "CARDS". You should also note that if you brought your EZPASS or SUN-PASS transponder from the USA it will not work.

TIP> On exiting the Autostrada, stay in your right lane if you want to use your credit card. If you have a problem paying the amount i.e. your credit card did not work, or whatever, the gate will automatically open. Once the gate opens, DO NOT DRIVE AWAY, if you take a look on the left you will see that the "remittance" machine (where you inserted your credit or debit card) has just spit out a long piece of paper. You need to grab this paper and pull over to the small building on the right. You will usually find parking behind the building.

You need to go inside with this piece of paper and your credit card and see the toll officer. If you don't pay the amount now, you will receive from your rental car company a notice that you did not pay your toll and they have charged your credit card the 25 Euro fee for doing all that research i.e. who drove the car that day. They then inform you that in a few weeks you will receive a formal invoice from the Autostrada people demanding payment. Sometimes they may add it on to the bill with the 25 Euros.

ITALY Over 300 Critical Tips

Now if you see the toll officer and present him with that strip of paper you can pay the toll on the spot and avoid that 25 Euro rental company fee. I know for sure they will take your credit or debit card. They probably will also take your good old fashion Euros. Make sure you save that receipt that you paid the toll and also stuff it in your passport wallet or your trip file.

TIP> If you want to pay in Euros look for the symbol of the hand and the coins.

TIP> Many of the newer toll booths accept all. Just keep your eyes open, but best is to stay in the far right hand lane.

TIP> Try not to fill up on the Autostrada where the prices are always higher. It is best to fuel up on exiting the Autostrada or late in the day.

TIP> Don't get stressed out when you see the price of fuel (gasoline or diesel). Remember you are on vacation (or holidays). Those prices you see are for liters not gallons... Yikes.

First gasoline and diesel is sold by the liter which is about a quart. Figure that there are about four liters (it's close enough) to the gallon. Then figure your exchange rate. So here is what you will pay for a gallon: Figure 130 Euros for a liter. Four of them are 520 Euors at an exchange rate of $1.20 for one Euro, you are paying about $6.24 per gallon. It is pricey, even if you are getting 40 miles to the gallon. A fill-up of a 12 gallon tank will cost you about $75. This is another item you might consider when comparing rail with renting a car.

TIP> When you are about 10 kilometers from the airport remember to fill up (or bring it back with a little more or the same amount you left with) else

they will charge you to refuel at a rate about 50% above what you would normally pay at the pump.

I usually fill it and top if off.   Also, I find it a bad idea to pre-pay for the gas when I rent the car. It is extremely difficult to bring it back empty!

TIP> And as a final tip. If you are staying at a hotel near the airport the night before your flight back to America or Canada (good idea), I suggest (if the hotel has a courtesy shuttle service) to drop the rental when you arrive at the airport the day before. We drop our bags at the hotel, check-in, drop the car at the airport then take the courtesy shuttle back to the hotel.

It all depends on the flight time.   However, using the above eliminates all that stress and may also save you a day of rental. And, remember if you are flying out of Rome, you will have to port your bags from the rental center in the garage to your check in counter in Terminal 1, 2 or 3. If you took the courtesy shuttle from the hotel they will drop you curbside.

CHAPTER 5

RAIL TRAVEL THROUGH ITALY

INTRODUCTION-

TIP> If you are considering any type of rail travel through Italy it is best to pick-up a copy of my book: *ITALY The Best Places to See by Rail.* **You will find it on Amazon.com and Barnes and Noble. You will find detailed rail itineraries, hotels and more tips just pertaining to rail travel. It's a worthwhile investment.**

Unlike the American rail system the Italian railway infrastructure was built and is owned by the federal government. This gives the Italian railway companies, both private and state owned, complete control over the operation of their trains. This is quite a difference between the USA, where with the exception of the Northeast Corridor (NEC), Amtrak uses private railroad tracks owned by the large freight railroads and not the government i.e. CSX, Union Pacific etc., to operate their trains.

Even though Amtrak trains are given a priority over freight trains, they usually, with the exception of the NEC, run dramatically several hours late. Delays of several hours to a full day late are rampant. On the other hand, Italian passenger trains run right on the clock.   If you are running late for a train and arrive about one minute after the published departure time (*partenze*), you will find the train has departed.   It is rare that trains ever run more than five minutes behind schedule.   Don't compare taking a slow and delayed Amtrak train across America with taking a rail trip through Italy.   They are totally different.   Take a look at the cover of my rail book.   That sleek *Frecciargento* ETR train will make the run from Rome to Florence in 90 minutes, averaging about 190 mph, and it won't be delayed.   Even Amtrak's Acela high speed trains operating on the NEC sometimes run behind schedule 30 minutes or more.   In summary, there is absolutely no comparison between Amtrak and the trains of Italy.   They are a world apart.

TIP> Most important tip on rail travel is that you must validate your rail ticket before departure. This is true for all regional trains.   If you have a reserved seat on a high speed inter-city train (not a regional slow train) you do not have to validate. The machines are on the platforms and are yellow or the newer type of blue/grey.
There is a stiff 50 Euro fine if you fail to validate. Sometimes, you can talk your way out of it and the train conductor will sign your ticket and give it back to you so you cannot use it again.

When placing your ticket in the machine to validate (frank it) you will hear the machine buzz and it will print the date and time on the edge of the ticket.

TIP if you are making connections and you are in doubt whether to validate or not, then validate. I would advise if you have two tickets to definitely

validate the second also. When in doubt ask the train conductor when he inspects your ticket on the first train.

TIP> Make sure you are on the correct platform. In large stations with many platforms you may be on the wrong platform.
The tracks are referred to as Binari. They are abbreviated as BIN on the signs at the stazione (station).

TIP> Several large stations have security checkpoints. One of them is Milan. You should allow extra time to clear security.

TIP> In general allow a minimum of 45 minutes before train departure to purchase your REGIONAL TICKETS. These are un-reserved seats.
You will have to queue up. Many times there are senior discounts and round trip specials. I have always found the automatic machines intimidating. Most of the rail stations are spelled in Italian of course. If you are not Italian, it's just a pain. I always go to the main counter.

TIP> Make sure you purchase round-trip tickets. Many times the small local stations are closed for tickets at certain times of the day or certain days of the week and you will be forced to pay a surcharge of one Euro on the train.

TIP> Most of the time you will find that a Eurail-Italy rail pass will NOT pay off at all.
A lot of people think a rail pass in Italy gives you unlimited travel via rail for say 30 days. It does not. The least expensive plan allows only 3 days in 30 days of travel. There are other plans. In pretty much all cases it will not pay off as opposed to buying point-to-point tickets.

You Need to Know Before You Go

Here is what you need to do to see if an Italy ONLY rail pass will be advantageous.

Go to the Trenitalia.com website. Then price out the tickets you will need. Then compare with getting a railpass. Remember, you still have to make a reservation for the fast (Frecci) trains. Also, the rail passes are not good on Italo. And of course, you don't want to use one of those rail pass days for a short trip of just 20 Euros round trip, for say Florence to Siena.

You can also divide the cost of the rail pass by the number of days and this will give you maximum for the day. For example if the 3 day pass is $127, that equates to about $42 per day.

The only way a rail pass will pay off is Venice to Palermo, Sicily on Day 1 of travel; Catania, Sicily to Milan on Day 2 of travel, Milan to Rome on Day 3 of travel. Since these are extremely long distances the cost of point to point tickets will be high. In this case an Italy Railpass will pay-off. So, do the math first.

TIP> When buying rail tickets always get the total "through rate"
What this means, is that if you have to make perhaps three connections to get from one place to another you ask for the through rate. For example: to the first connection is 5 Euros, the second 8 Euros and the third leg 4 Euros. That's a total of 17 Euros. However, you will find the through rate is 14 Euros. If you are travelling from Florence to Manarola (one of the five towns of the Cinque Terre) do not purchase a ticket from Florence to La Spezia and then from La Spezia to Manarola. You should purchase a ticket from Florence to Manarola.

TIP> Always arrive at major train stations at least 30 minutes before train departure; better would be 45 minutes or more, if you have to purchase tickets.
The major stations are classified by the Italian Rail System (RFI) as Platinum stations:

ITALY Over 300 Critical Tips

They are Bari Centrale, Bologna Centrale, Firenze-SMN, Genova Piazza Principe, Genova Brignole, Milano Centrale, Milano Porta Garibaldi, Napoli Centrale, Padova, Palermo Centrale, Roma Ostiense, Roma Termini, Roma Tiburtina, Torino Porta Nuova, Venezia Santa Lucia, Venezia Mestre and Verona Porta Nuova.

TIP> If you are on a long haul train (a Frecci or an Italo) where the travel times exceeds 90 minutes make sure you arrive with another 15 minutes to spare and explore the main rail station and get some food to go (they call it take-away).
A Panini on the train which was made about 8-10 hours prior to departure will cost you about 10 Euros. That same Panini made fresh at the train station will cost you seven Euros or less.

TIP> Keep your eyes on the electronic train boards in these major stations. In most stations, they will only post the train Binari twenty minutes before departure. Do not attempt to go down to the platform earlier since you may get on another train going somewhere else. Wait until the train is posted.

TIP> If you are travelling on a regional train (not a high speed "Frecci" or an Italo) make sure you are sitting in the correct coach i.e. first class or second class. Note some coaches are actually split. First class sit on the forward part of the coach and second class sit in the rear of the coach. They are usually separated by the toilets. Frecci's and Italo trains usually have separate coaches for second and first class.
If you are caught in first class and only have a second class ticket, you will be fined on the spot!

You Need to Know Before You Go

The reverse is true but no fine. If you hold a first class ticket you can certainly sit in the second class coach

TIP> If you are running late to your train and you have a   reserved seat in a coach, you need to hop on the coach and "walk the train". What I mean is just walk from car to car in the train till you get to the proper coach and find your seat. If you are late and trying to find your coach from the platform, you may find that the train is leaving without you.

TIP>   mind your carry-ons. On local or regional trains there may be unscrupulous (pickpockets) on the train. They will walk the train looking for items they can pick in a hurry then jump off the train before it leaves the platform.   Never leave your carry-ons to visit the café or the toilet without someone you know or another tourist couple to watch them.

Make sure you keep all carry-ons zipped and avoid placing the smaller ones on the baggage racks near the doors. Keep them in the overhead racks or the "V" area between the seats.

TIP> And, as a final point you should be aware that labor strikes are a fact of life in Italy. Either the garbage collectors are on strike or it's something else. Strikes by rail employees are common. Here is what you need to do:

Unlike the USA all employees do not strike at the same time. So you will see posted signs i.e. "there will be a strike of train conductors on November 10, 2020." If you consult the internet you will see that some trains will be cancelled.   Either hopefully you have left Italy and are back in the USA, or you need to go to the train station and exchange your ticket for another train that will be operating. This most of the time affects the Intercity trains i.e. the Frecci's and other trains operated by Italo.

CHAPTER 6

MEALS AND RESTAURANTS
FOOD FOR THOUGHT

At this chapter you are probably thinking, why do we need any tips on this subject at all. Yes, I know it may be easier to eat spaghetti by twirling it with a fork in a spoon. But seriously are there any real tips here? The answer is yes. And here they are:

TIP> You will always find the best food and the best prices where the locals go.
Always ask the desk clerk or the concierge where *they* go for dinner or lunch. Many times they will point you in the direction where they go. Make sure you get the name of the restaurant on a piece of paper so you can show it to someone if you are lost. Many times they will not post the menu outside (see below) instead they will display it on a chalk board. And many of the local places will not take credit cards. However, the food will be just as good if not better than the touristy places.

If you do go to the where the locals go, make sure you bring an Italian to English dictionary with you with a good "menu" section. And, remember Scaloppini Miale is pork scaloppini not veal scaloppini. Also you can't go wrong with the fish of the day (pesce del giorno). You will always know that you are getting something really fresh. And, further don't be afraid to ask for another basket of bread. No big deal.

TIP> I strongly recommend that you read the menu before you enter the restaurant

You Need to Know Before You Go

Italian (at least Rome) law states that all restaurants, cafes, etc. must post their menu with prices on the outside of the establishment. Before you walk into an establishment or sit down on the outside café for a drink, you must be aware of the prices they will charge.

On a recent tour of mine to Italy, two gentlemen were annoyed when they received the bill for two drinks and a Panini while having lunch in front of a swanky hotel overlooking the Grand Canal in Venice. They could not believe it. Get this, two Paninis, two imported bottles of beer, a "grande" bottle of water and of course the cover charge. The bill was a little over $50. What they failed to do is read the posted menu before sitting down. A few blocks back without a view of the Grand Canal that same lunch would have cost $25.

TIP> You can't avoid this. However, every order whether you are one person or two people at a table will be assessed a cover charge (coperto). This charge can be anywhere from 2 Euros to 5 Euros per person. What?
It's automatic. You can't say you don't want it. If you don't want to pay for it, simply get up and leave. It includes, get this ... the table cloth, the napkins, the bread, the olive oil and if you are lucky a small plate of olives. Even if you are having lunch and you have a table cloth, a basket of break, the olive oil, you will pay a cover charge. If you are at a snack bar, sit at a table with no table cloth and they bring over no bread, you will probably not receive a cover charge.

In restaurants in Rome they will ask you if you want bread. The cover charge will vary depending on your bread requirements.

Sometimes they will assess you a separate cover charge, in addition to the regular cover charge for bread. This is called a "pane e coperto". Hmmm this may be getting complex.

ITALY Over 300 Critical Tips

TIP>   Don't get bent out of shape when you read the menu and see the prices.   They include the VAT (Value Added Tax) and get this... the service charge what we in the USA and Canada call the TIP (To Insure Promptness).

TIP> It is customary to leave a few coins on the table if the food and service was exceptional.

TIP> I suggest you drop one Euro for each 15 Euros you spend.

TIP> No need to order bottled water in Rome, it's perfectly safe. However, if you want the water with the bubbles in it you will need to order *acqua minerale con gas*. It comes in a bottle, except if you live in New York City where it comes out of the tap.

TIP> It is usually normal to order a bottle of water with gas (con gas) or without gas (sin gas) at dinner since restaurants don't pour tap water out of a pitcher. Bottled water is relatively cheap and will cost you 2-4 Euros depending on the size of the bottle. You can also take the bottle home with you if you don't consume it all.

TIP> If you are going to dinner where the tourists go, don't feel intimidated when you order a "first", say an antipasto or a fried calamari and a main dish, say some fish or meat, and the wait person looks at you and says "no pasta"?
What this means is that you are not ordering "pasta". I mean the traditional comfort food of Italy. Made so many ways and made the Italian way. It's okay. Don't cave in. Just tell them you are on a diet and you can't eat all that great Italian food. He will understand. And, don't order another basket of bread!

You Need to Know Before You Go

TIP> It is best to order, a starter (appetizer) , a pasta and a second (main dish) then look at the waiter and say "we are going to split it". In this way you will also have room for a salad and/or dessert. You can also add another appetizer and enjoy more of that great Italian food and still have room for "Dolce" (dessert).

TIP> In Italy your salad is usually served after the primary dish, just before the dessert. Don't think the wait person forgot something. Often times they will ask you "do you want your salad first or last"?

TIP> The locals in Italy, like many other med countries eat late, usually around 7:30PM or better at 8PM. If you arrive about 7PM you may find the restaurant closed. Best is to find an enoteca (wine bar) and have a glass of wine while you wait till your restaurant of choice opens.

TIP> After serving any dish or course, if there is something wrong with it e.g. the pasta is mush and not "al dente" say something immediately and the wait person will take care of it. And always thank him after he returns with the new serving.

TIP> Don't expect the waiter to bring over the bill after you finish your meal. They won't. They view it as "un-polite". After you are finished and ready to leave, you must summon the waitperson with a gesture and the words "il conto per favore".

TIP> Don't get bent out of shape like a piece of limp Tagliatelle when you request the bill (il conto) it may take 30-45 minutes to get it. It is best to request the bill after you order the meal and get a head start on it, just kidding of course. Just have another cup of coffee, decaf of course as you wait for the il conto.

TIP> Don't be alarmed if you order Cappuccino and the waiter does a double-take. Italians rarely order Cappuccino after dinner. The same rule applies to hot chocolate which you usually order at a café or a standup bar. By the way, you ought to try it. It's more like chocolate pudding than our watery hot chocolate which is made with milk.

TIP> As stated previously and mandatory at most eating establishments, if you want to use your credit or debit card you need to SHOW it to the wait person who in turn will bring over a machine and allow you to conduct the transaction at your table. If they don't bring over the machine or you can't use it at the reception desk, it is best to pay cash.

TIP> Also remember that all prices include the service charge. If your wait person says it does not, he is giving you a run for your money.
In fact, if you don't believe him/her about the tip being included, you will find nowhere on the credit card receipt to insert it like we do in the USA or Canada. When leaving, drop a few coins on the table.

TIP> You must have in your possession the receipt for your dinner or lunch and further carry it for at least 100 meters (figure one football field). Huh?
You are probably wondering what this silly rule is. Get this, it's not a rule, it's a law. There are two reasons for it. First the federal government of Italy imposes a VAT (Value Added Tax) on practically everything sold including many services. In other words they are taxing at the consumption level. I might note that Italy also has a personal income tax, just like the USA

and Canada. Italy like many countries in Europe (and elsewhere), has a staggering cash economy i.e. in other words "pay me cash" and no tax. In the USA we refer to this as "pay me under the table". To prevent this and ensure that VAT is collected, Italy has the Financial Guard (Guardia di Finanza) in addition to the local police.

If you look at any receipt it will have the VAT number printed on it. If a policeman stops you on exiting a restaurant or someone from the Financial Guard and you do not have this printed receipt, he or she may cite you or better fine the restaurant. These Financial Guards run around in little white cars. They also perform many of the functions of our Coast Guard i.e. combat drug smuggling, money laundering, etc. In my thirty plus trips to Italy, I have never been stopped once. So don't worry. Just make sure you keep your receipts. Also, it is rumored that in some jurisdictions they have dropped this requirement of carrying your receipt.

TIP> Unlike America where I usually figure 90 minutes to have a sit down dinner, you will find service rather slow. Do not get upset about this. It is their norm. You should anticipate a minimum of two hours to have dinner.

In most places, everything is cooked to order. They usually don't even have salads or antipasto's ready to go like in the USA where they are premade and kept in refrigerators with plastic wrap over them.

TIP> Don't complain about the poor service and don't get "antsy or testy" and let the other people know in the restaurant. This is rude. Service in Italy is always slow. You will also find that the number of tables assigned to a wait person is about twice that of the United States. In addition, if you

frequent the local eateries (not where the tourists go) you will find many times that the owners kid's help out with serving or the bussing of the tables.

TIP> If you spot a "stand-up" bar and you want to order perhaps a Panini and an Americano Coffee and take it to a table on the sidewalk outside, you will pay more. So best is consuming it at the bar.

That's right. An Americano Coffee at the bar will cost you perhaps two Euros.   However, if you sit down or have it delivered to you via a wait person or the bartender it will cost you three Euros.

It is best to look at the menu card usually posted outside. You will see two columns; one for the stand-up bar price and the other for the table price.

If you want to do "Nada" i.e. sit at a table and do some people watching or whatever, you will pay more for all the food. However, if you order it at the bar and consume it at the bar, it will cost you a lot less.

TIP> If you want to be away from the smokers you need to sit inside the restaurant. They still allow smoking outside.

You should bear in mind that most of Europe still smokes. Italy does not have a surgeon general. Give it a couple of years.

# # #

CHAPTER 7

ROME & THE VATICAN

INTRODUCTION-
This chapter supplements TIPs in the Itineraries Chapter.

---------- ROME ----------

Rome, also known as the "eternal city" is truly a walking city. In one day I have walked from the Spanish Steps to the Vatican Museum and then back to the Coliseum, I was bushed!

Rome is a hodgepodge of historical monuments. It's like someone put them all in one of those old time muskets, pulled the trigger and splattered them all over the place. It is a mix of sites from ancient Roman times to the Renaissance to modern times. There is no rhyme or reason where they are located. The monument to King Victor Emmanuel II was completed in 1935 and is located one football field from Trajan's market built in 100AD and the Roman Forum built in the 7th Century BC.

Around Rome it is hard to discern exactly what monument goes with what event or time frame. For example, the Spanish Steps were built in 1717 and there was no historical event associated with them, likewise for Trevi Fountain, 1762.

TIP> If you plan on going on any of the 3 or 4 hour tours, take a good look at the brochures or the websites. Many tours "view" different sites e.g. The Borghese Gardens, Trajan's Market, etc., but do not "visit". If it says "visit", the coach will stop

93

and you will be escorted into the site for a narration.

TIP> If you are taking one of the 3-4 hour tours you will be given a radio receiver and "ear buds" to carry with you. You will receive a live narration of the site you are visiting by your tour guide. Do not under any circumstances loose the receiver. There is a charge of up to $100 if you don't turn in your unit at the end of the tour. And yes, they will charge it on your credit card.

TIP> Before I discuss Rome, it is best that you print out a map (at least of the Historic District) and on the other side of the river, The Vatican. Or you can purchase one of those laminated "Streetwise Rome" maps (ISBN-13: 978-2067229815) from Amazon for about $9. It is worth its weight in gold. I find it very difficult to carry around a heavy tour book and view the separate maps. Many times I will take a photo using my smartphone of a certain map.

TIP> Most of the historical district of Rome encompasses a square of about one mile. What you need to do, forgetting the Vatican City, is put dots at the places you wish to visit. Then all you need do is connect all the dots so as to minimize the walking distance. Do not include the Vatican as it will be discussed later.

TIP> If you have a smartphone or a mini-tablet, use Google Maps and preload your step by step directions using WIFI at your hotel.

TIP> See if you can make the dots a circle so you don't have to double track back on the same route.

You Need to Know Before You Go

TIP> If you have purchased tickets for the Forum and Coliseum make sure you will arrive in the proper time slot.
If you arrive too early you will have to wait until your time slot.

TIP> From my tour days, I recommend the first full day in Rome be reserved for what I call the walking tour of Rome i.e. "Monumental Rome". It is best to reserve the second full day for the Vatican Museum in the morning, lunch and then the Coliseum and Forum for 2-3PM on. At the end of the day best to take a taxi or the Metro back to your hotel if you are too bushed to enjoy the walk.

TIP> On your arrival day in Rome, if you are taking that Hop-on-Hop-off bus, take notes on the route of the bus i.e. the order of the monuments the driver passes. If you do not want to jot them down then record them on your smartphone.

TIP> At a minimum the major sites you should *visit* (with the exception of the Coliseum and the Forum) are:
  Trevi Fountain
  Pantheon
  Spanish Steps
  Piazza Navona
  Castel Saint' Angelo (can also be visited on
     Vatican day)

TIP> Secondary sites to visit are:
  The Baths of Caracalla
  The Circus Maximus
  The Catacombs of Rome (there are several)

TIP> Consider signing up on the internet for a walking tour of the Historic District. This will cost you less than $10. However, bear in mind that it is highly regimented.

TIP> Many shops close down from 1-4PM. You may want to plan on lunch about 1-2PM. However, in the highly touristed areas i.e. at the bottom of the Spanish Steps along the Via Condotti, you will find most shops open. If you are staying in one of the local areas i.e. Trastevere, Flaminia, or EUR most of the shops will be closed as well as the other residential areas.

TIP> Consider taking the Metro (there are only three lines) to Spagna, (The Piazza di Spagna) and the Spanish Steps. The TIP here is that there is an elevator from the Metro which will take you to the top of the steps located on Via Sistina next to the Trinita dei Monti church, so you won't have to walk up them. Follow the signs.

TIP> Located only four blocks from the Coliseum, is one of Michelangelo's greatest works.... "The Moses". Few people know that it is so close and there is no fee to view this incredible marble sculpture. It is hidden. Here is how you find it:
First locate the Coliseum Metro Station. Then look to the right of it and you will spot the Oppio Caffe. Now to the right of it is a large park (Parco del Colle Oppio). Walk up (it's a slight hill) the Via delle Terme di Tito. In two blocks when the road takes a sharp right, take a left on that small street (note the bar on the left). Follow the walking crowd for about two more blocks to the Basilica di San Pietro in Vincoli (St. Peter in Chains). Enter the Basilica and view The Moses. And yes, he chiseled this whole thing out of one massive block of marble, and yes with no power tools!

You Need to Know Before You Go

TIP> For one of the most historical cities in the world, Rome is short on public toilets. And in fact, a lot of them you and I would not use, even in an emergency. And don't ask me why they don't have toilet seats. I don't know the answer to this either. However, you will note a shortage of Home Depot's and Lowes store's in Italy.

Many of the smaller hotels in the historical district usually do not allow "outsiders" to use their toilets which are located   off the reception area. However, it is perfectly acceptable to duck into a "stand-up" bar, order a café or an American Café first, then ask to use the bathroom i.e. "Dough vey e banyos".   Oh, and remember to pay for that café, just nod and the barista will tell you it's only one Euro. And, make sure you say "Grazie".

TIP> Rome municipal regulations state that you cannot eat sitting or standing on the Spanish Steps. In other words if you sit down on the steps, bite into your Panini or whatever and a policemen sees you, you may be fined.

TIP> There are numerous roof top restaurants and bars in Rome and near Vatican City. Instead of having a pricy dinner you should consider going to one of these rooftop bars for a drink around sunset.

---------- **THE VATICAN CITY** ----------

INTRODUCTION-

You should note that the Vatican (The Holy See) is NOT part of Rome or Italy or the Province of Lazio. It is a separate country created in 1929 by the Lateran Treaty. It has its own security force as no Rome or Italian police are allowed behind the walls or in St. Peter's Square. In addition, it has its own post office, radio/TV station and a pharmacy. Full time population is about 600. It is one of the smallest (if not the smallest) country in the world. It is best that you view it as an island in the city of Rome.

The Swiss Guards you will see are exactly what they are. They are photographed in their colorful outfits and their "halberds" thousands of times a day. The Holy See (short for Holy City and other terms) has its own armed and uniformed military in addition to the Swiss Guards, police and security personnel. The Swiss Guards guard the main gates to the Vatican City and also participate in ceremonial functions for the Pope.

The Vatican City has four major components: The Vatican Museum, Vatican Gardens, Basilica of St. Peter's and St. Peter's Square. There are also minor items to visit if you can. They are the "scavi" beneath the Basilica, the dome which you climb via an elevator and stairs and the railroad station (which is closed to tourists).

As previously discussed in the Itineraries Chapter, you need to book your Vatican Museum tickets (which also includes the Vatican Gardens) several months before leaving your home town, else you will wait on a very long line about 1-2 hours.

You Need to Know Before You Go

TIP> The most critical tip on visiting the Vatican is proper dress. I have seen many people rejected at security trying to enter St. Peter's with flip-flops, tank tops or shorts. You get the point.

You can check the Vatican's website for proper dress. However, here is the basic rule which applies to men and women: You must cover your knees and your shoulders. I suggest long skirts or pants for the ladies; hats for ladies is optional. Men certainly can wear hats.

TIP> I always suggest to visit the Vatican Museum in the morning when you have a lot of energy, then visit St. Peter's afterwards. There is an awful lot of walking in the Museum.

TIP> On entering the Vatican Museum there is a major security check. Avoid bringing any backpacks. You can check them, but you may not be coming back through the security checkpoint area (see TIP below). So it is best that you do not take them on your Vatican day.

TIP> You cannot take any pen knives or any type of food, etc. into the Vatican Museum. You must check them at the cloakroom before passing through security. The security checkpoint is almost identical to the airport security; except you will not have to remove your belt (for the men) and your shoes. This is important since many of you will probably not pass this way again. See the next TIP.

First to view the ceiling of the Sistine Chapel which was painted by Michelangelo in the years 1508-1512 you must walk about one quarter mile through the main gallery of the Vatican Museum and then climb a staircase (there are elevators). There is more walking once you climb those stairs. Be extra street savvy walking the galleries in the Museum.

ITALY Over 300 Critical Tips

The main gallery of the Museum is like a long subway tunnel. Very few people actually stop to view the sculptures, stone carvings, tapestries and other items the Vatican has collected over 400 years. They are all going to one place... to view the ceiling of The Sistine Chapel.

During your walk you will notice Official Vatican Guides giving explanations of the gifts to the Vatican: tapestries, ancient "findings" and paintings. This walk will take you about 30 minutes. Once again be "street savvy". You should then figure another 15 minutes before you enter the Sistine Chapel.

Once entering the Chapel you cannot use your camera's flash to take any pictures and there is strict silence. There are numerous security personnel in the chapel monitoring the strict rules for the viewing.

The ceiling has many panels and there is also the painting of *The Last Judgment* above the altar. And, no Michelangelo did not paint the ceiling frescoes' lying on his back as seen in the movie *"The Agony and the Ecstasy"*.

After viewing the ceiling frescoes and the painted walls you must exit the Chapel of either two ways:

TIP> On exiting the Sistine Chapel there are two doors on the exit side. You should exit the Chapel on the right hand side "Solo Gruppo" (groups only) if you want to avoid the 45 minute walk back to the main entrance of the Museum where you entered and passed through security. However, if you want to have lunch before going over to St. Peter's Basilica or have checked items in the cloakroom, then walk back to the Museum entrance and check-in security via the left hand door.

You Need to Know Before You Go

TIP> From a timing standpoint, it is best to visit the Vatican Museum with its Sistine Chapel then exit via the special stairway for groups only, visit the Church (see separate TIP below) and then exit the Church and head for the Borgo Pio for lunch.

TIP> If you are trying to exit via the Chapel's right hand door en route to the Church and are challenged by the security personnel who sometimes are dressed in "tails and a high hat" just tell him that you were separated from your group which is on their way to St. Peter's. He will open the door to the stairway and usher you out of the Chapel. Just follow the staircase out of the building then the exterior stairway. The outdoor stairway will drop you directly into the secured area of St. Peter's Square next to the men's and ladies room. You will not have to go through the St. Peter's Basilica security checkpoint and possibly queue.

If you exit on the left accidentally, you will be forced to walk the entire length of the Vatican Museum and exit where you entered. It is best to skip down to the TIP on having lunch on the Borgo Pio.

TIP> After using the facilities (suggested) you may enter St. Peter's Basilica. It is best to walk counter-clockwise through the church. Start at Michelangelo's "Pieta" and work your way around. The "Pieta", like the "Moses" was chiseled out of one large block of marble; and once again there were no power tools to do it. It will be on your right as you enter. By the way, if you see those Pope's under glass, you are correct; they have been dead a few hundred years.

TIP> I am repeating part of this TIP from the Itineraries Chapter. If you are looking for excellent places to have lunch, need more exercise (or the Vatican Museum was not enough), as you exit the Museum from where you came in, follow the wall to your right for about one quarter mile until you reach the Borgo Pio on your left. You can't miss it. Look for the Sant' Anna gates to the Vatican and those colorful Swiss Guards on your right. On the Borgo Pio and the small cross streets you will find over 50 restaurants. They are all competitively priced and not a lot of money. The Borgo Pio extends from the wall of the Vatican City all the way down to the Tiber River, a distance of about 7 blocks. Toward the Tiber you will also find many outdoor cafes for lunch. After lunch you are free to visit St. Peter's Basilica. See my TIP above on how to tour the largest church in the world. Also note, you will have to go through security again.

TIP> There is a cafeteria in the Vatican Museum near the gardens. However, there are many negative comments and I have only eaten there once; not recommended. You will have a better experience on the Borgo Pio.

TIP> If you want to climb to the top of St. Peter's Basilica, you can. There are two options, one is to climb to the inside and look into the Church or better climb onto the outside roof and view the square and the skyline of Rome. There is always a line. You might consider before you set off for your day trip of Monumental room to head over to the Vatican and climb to the roof at 8AM when it opens. Else, if you have a third day in Rome, consider doing the climb.

St. Peter's Basilica is the tallest structure in Rome (of course it's actually in Vatican City). Like Washington DC, and its Capitol Building, no building can be taller than it.

You Need to Know Before You Go

In fact, if you get to St. Peter's at 7:45AM when there is no line, you probably will have enough time to get back to your hotel to enjoy breakfast; else, you will have to settle for a Cappuccino at a standup bar with a pastry or a grilled breakfast Panini.

You purchase the tickets at the Basilica. As of this writing in 2020 it is 10 Euros with the elevator and 8 Euros without the elevator. It is best to consult the internet for all the details. And, yes, I climbed it in August 1987 with my oldest son, Scott.

TIP> If you are really into history, you might want to consider a "SCAVI TOUR" of St. Peter's. This is actually under the Basilica. I believe this is the Latin root for the term "scavenger" i.e. scavenger hunt. You will definitely see the "leftovers" in the Scavi of St. Peter's.
This is a special tour which you must book in advance, at least 90 days or more. There is a charge and only small groups are taken on the tour. The scavi contains the tombs of prior Pope's and supposedly St. Peter himself. There are lots of other artifacts in the scavi.

TIP> You may want to have a narrated tour of St. Peter's. If not, it is perfectly okay to do your own circular walk in the largest church in the world. Make sure you definitely view Michelangelo's "The Pieta", as discussed above. It is best to consult the tour books for the details. You need to allow a minimum of one hour to "walk" the church.

TIP> Avoid visiting St. Peter's on a Sunday when there are many masses in different languages. The place is a zoo. However, on Sunday do consider if you are of the Catholic Faith and you wish to attend a mass. You should check times for English.

ITALY Over 300 Critical Tips

TIP> Consider a once in a lifetime experience of attending "The Angelus". This occurs on Sunday's when the Pope appears from the window of his apartment and delivers a short talk and then blesses the crowd in St. Peter's Square. Check on-line if he will be in residence and the exact time. You should arrive 30 minutes prior.

TIP> On special Sundays and certain holidays, the Vatican Museum is free to visit. While it is free, be advised that the crowds are overwhelming.

CHAPTER 8

FLORENCE-FIRENZE

INTRODUCTION-

Florence (Firenze) is considered the city of the Renaissance i.e. the rebirth of the arts and sciences. If you remember your history, the Roman Empire fell in 476AD. After that, for about 500 years there were no new scientific developments and no creations of art. Basically Europe slept for 500 years.

Several hundred years later about 800-1000AD the dark ages (sometimes called the Middle Ages) saw the birth of the feudal system. We all know the history here: castles, marauding tribes, lords, serfs, etc.

About 1400AD, Europe in particular, began to emerge from the Dark Ages and the saw the beginnings of the Italian City States i.e. Venice, Florence, Rome, etc. These City States eventually merged to become the Republic of Italy. I won't go into all that history about Garibaldi, the Medici's, etc., because it is not the intent of this book.

The reason I bring this up is that just like the modern city of Rome reflects ancient Rome and the Roman

ITALY Over 300 Critical Tips

Empire, Florence reflects a snapshot of the Italian Renaissance with buildings, bridges, churches and her preservation of the masterpieces of the famous Italian artists.

TIP> Before you book that hotel in Florence, consider staying in a town about 50 minutes (by rail) due west of Florence known as Montecatini Terme. If you drive, it's only 30 minutes. Why do I recommend Montecatini Terme? It's simple. It will cost you a lot less, it is more central to Pisa, Lucca the Cinque Terre, etc. and if you are driving, there is free parking at most of the hotels. A typical four star hotel in Montecatini will cost you about one third the price you will pay in Florence. In addition you won't have to pay to park your chariot each night, and you won't wind up in a ZTL.
There are two trains every hour to and from Florence and the fare is only $7 each way. No parking hassles, no ZTL zones and no crazy drivers.

The town is the home of the famous "baths" e.g. like Baden-Baden, Germany. And would you believe there are over 400 hotels in this little town of only 20,000 people.

In addition to staying in a more central place, the town is absolutely a delight to walk in, even after dark. There is a large park with a kid's playing area. There are plenty of restaurants and there are even two rail stations, one on each side of the town. In addition there are lots of restaurants and shops, not to mention a few grocery stores right in town.

You can take the funicular to the top of the old town, known as Montecatini Alto. It is best at sunset where you can enjoy a gelato, a late lunch or an aperitif before you head back to your hotel for a well deserved nap. You may even want to have

You Need to Know Before You Go

dinner in Montecatini Alto as you watch the twinkling lights of the town below.

If you are looking for an excellent four star hotel right in the center of town, I recommend the Hotel Puccini (named after the composer). Please give my best to Pasquale the owner and do book directly.

If you are thinking about visiting Siena, Lucca, Pisa, The Cinque Terre, San Gimignano and more, consider renting a furnished apartment in Montecatini Terme. This works out usually best for 5-7 days. It is great for a family and you get the experience of living in an Italian town and shopping with the locals, etc. I cannot tell you enough about this town and its central park and baths. It is one of my favorites.

TIP> As discussed in the Itineraries Chapter, you should plan on several extra days in Florence (or Montecatini Terme) to make day trips to Siena, San Gimignano, Pisa, Lucca and the Cinque Terre.

TIP> As I also stated in the Itineraries Chapter, it is best to get your tickets to the "DAVID" and the Uffizi Gallery at least 90 days prior to your departure for Italy else you will wait 1-2 hours.

TIP> If you are arriving by train in Florence's Santa Maria Novella station, be aware of scammers who will want to carry your bags to your hotel and/or give you a free tour of the historic district. Just keep on walking!

TIP> If you have seen Rome on a prior visit to Italy and want to visit Florence and then Venice, you can usually fly into Florence via a connection in Europe. The same is true for Pisa. However, if flying into Pisa you need to take a bus or the train to Florence,

ITALY Over 300 Critical Tips

about an hour away. As of this writing in 2020 there are no non-stops to either Pisa or Florence from the USA or Canada.

TIP> You should consider for your full second, third and fourth day in Florence the 72 hour Firenzecard. However, I must admit to you I have never found this card to be of any value because: It is not valid for the Accademia to see "David" or the Uffizi Gallery to see the treasures of the Renaissance. It does not give you access to visit the Cupola of the Duomo, however, for all the other museums and there are plenty, you gain free admission and you do not have to wait in any lines.

TIP> See the Itineraries Chapter for a detail of the one day walking tour of Florence. Here is a quick recap with a little more that can be accomplished in a day:

    10AM See the David at the Academy
    11AM Walk over to the Dumo and do visit
          the "Scavi" below (it' free) directly
          next to the book store.
    1PM   Enjoy lunch at the Piazza Signoria
    3PM   Walk a few blocks over to the Nuovo
          Mercado for souvenir shopping.
          Here, you will find some real good
          deals on leather items, etc. It's
          a good place to haggle if you are
          buying a lot of items.

Now turn around and walk to the river (It's the Arno) and follow the crowd to the Ponte Vecchio Bridge. Here you will find lots and lots of jewelry stores. However, I can tell you that I have never found any bargains here. Continue and cross the bridge to the other side of town, known as

You Need to Know Before You Go

"Oltrarno" and if time permits visit the Boboli Gardens and the Pitti Palace.

TIP> After the Ponte Vecchio bridge consider doubling back to the Duomo and climb the Cupola for a sunset view of Firenze. Hopefully about sunset the crowd has simmered down and you will be able to climb to the top (if you have the energy). You will need to buy your tickets online also before you leave the USA or Canada. Consult the internet for the timed tickets.

CHAPTER 9

VENICE

INTRODUCTION-

I love Venice! In fact, I love Amsterdam and Bruges. All three of course are "canal" towns. However, nothing compares to the medieval city built in a lagoon in the Adriatic ocean about one thousand years ago. The place is mindboggling with about 120 islands connected by over 400 bridges.

On the other hand I have heard as many negative comments about Venice as I have heard positive comments. Comments range from very dirty, hordes of crowds to "hold on to your wallet" and watch out for those pigeon droppings.

What I like best about Venice is that there is no other place like it in the world. Nothing can compare. However, Venice is decaying rapidly. It is sinking into the muck below. In recent years the cruise ships coming and going at the rate of 1-2 each day have done a number on the buildings in the Lagoon. As I write this book there is a plan to move the cruise terminal to Marghera which is next to Venice Mestre on the mainland. A new cruise terminal will be built. Ships will not navigate the Grand Canal in front of St. Mark's Piazza. But, instead will take a different, non-picturesque route to the new location.

TIP> Watch your dates you expect to be in Venice. If it's Venice Carnival time, you could be shut out of a hotel room, even in Venice Mestre.

You Need to Know Before You Go

TIP> If it's Venice Carnival time (yes where they wear those leather masks and outfits) you should consider staying in Padua.
Padua is only 28 minutes away by train. There are some excellent hotels next to the rail station and very large hotels downtown.

If all fails, try the hotels in Venice di Jesolo. It's a short bus trip ride away and off season you may find some hotels that are open. The place is family and kid friendly and hosts lots of hotels and motels, many on the beach. In season, there are fast ferries to the Lagoon.

TIP> This is a real big tip. Don't put off seeing Venice. If you do put if off for say ten or twenty years, it may be under water.

TIP> Before committing to a few nights in Venice consider a day trip from Florence.
If you go for the day you can find Frecci and Italo trains about 7-9AM which make the 2.25 hour run for about 40 Euros (one way). You can see the highlights of Venice (see below) and then come back in the evening.

Bear in mind that you can't wake up at the last minute while on that extra day in Florence. The morning and evening trains are usually booked solid when reservations open up 90 days prior. So remember, you are not the only person in the world that thought about doing a day trip to Venice. If you wind up taking a local regional train you will be spending about three hours on a sloooooo..train, and yes that's each way.

Now on with my other tips.

TIP> If you are flying into Venice, your best way to get from Marco Polo Airport to the Lagoon (Piazzale

ITALY Over 300 Critical Tips

Roma) or Venice Mestre is the ATVO bus. It operates every 20 minutes and costs only 8 Euros.
If you want to spend big bucks on a transfer from Marco Polo Airport, there are water taxis. Cost is about 115 Euros. Yikes, a lot of money for a speedboat ride of 20 minutes! You do need to make a reservation. There are several operators. Most of them will take you directly to your hotel. There are restrictions due to some hotels and fog in the evening.

The ATVO bus is express and will take you directly to the Piazzale Roma and runs every 20 minutes. There may be a quick one minute stop in Mestre opposite the rail station. However, sometimes buses go only to Mestre. If you are transferring to a train (to go to Rome, Florence, Paris or where ever) do ask the driver if the bus stops at Mestre Stazione. You can pay onboard. If you are bound for the Lagoon you should arrive at the Piazzale Roma in twenty minutes. You will have to port your bags to your hotel or hire a porter (see the Itineraries Chapter).

A taxi to Piazzale Roma from the airport will cost you about 35-45 Euros. Private car transfers are also available. Price ranges from $45-90. However, remember that they can't take you directly to your hotel (unless it is in Mestre), only to the Piazzale Roma where you must walk to your hotel. And, yes, there are many bridges over the canals.

TIP> If you are staying in Mestre, make sure you inform the taxi driver with the hotel name so he/she does not take you to the Piazzale Roma accidently.

TIP> If you are trying to save a lot of walking, consider a hotel within two blocks of a Vaporetto (waterbus) stop.
It is best to use Google Maps and bring up a detailed map of Venice. Note the Vaporetto stops and the hotels. If you

112

compare this with hotels on booking.com (select "show on map") you can see where the hotels are with respect to the Vaporetto stops.

TIP> I am putting this tip high on the list since it is really critical and most tourists do fall into this trap. You cannot feed the pigeons anymore in St. Mark's square. This means no nuts, no breadcrumbs leftover from breakfast or anything,... nada.
The law was enacting in 2018. There is now a stiff fine (may be paid on the spot) of 50 Euros. If you see a police officer (probably wears a white hat) approaching you, it's probably too late. The best is to plead ignorance and see if you can wiggle your way out of this.

TIP> Consult my chapter on Itineraries for more TIPs on Venice. What follows is additional tips.

TIP> If a pigeon decides to do a "dive bomb" on you and poops; do not attempt to clean the poop off. Wait till it dries and then just brush the dried flakes off with a credit card. When you get back to your hotel remove the remainder with a wet cloth.
Also, remember to wash that credit card before putting it back in your wallet. And do put that washcloth on the floor with the rest of the soiled linens.

TIP> Venice is a maze. The best thing to do if you are lost is to take a look at the corners of most buildings. At about 10 feet up you will see black letters painted with arrows. They usually read: "FERROVIA- The rail station Santa Lucia, "SAN MARCO" (yes, where the bulk of the pigeons hang out) and "RIALTO" (the Rialto Bridge and Market).
If you keep reading these signs from one point to another you will find your way where ever you are going. Many times you will be able to get from one place to another in several different

ITALY Over 300 Critical Tips

ways. Also, forget those maps. Just navigate by the building signs and follow the crowds.

TIPS> Many of the walkways in Venice are tight alleys. Be extra cautious as there may be pickpockets lurking.
Suggest you keep your hand in your pocket on your wallet and ladies mind your bags. See the Security Chapter for more TIPs.

Also, when walking over any bridges keep to the right and hug the handrail. It's more secure from a security standpoint and also from being knocked over.

TIP> The best deal going in Venice is the #2 Vaporetto or waterbus. It traverses the entire route of the Grand Canal. A ticket good for 75 minutes of unlimited travel will cost you 7.50 Euros.

TIP> You do not have to purchase a ticket for a child who is UNDER 6 years of age.

TIP> If you do not have a ticket you can board the Vaporetto but you must see the "conductor" IMMEDIATELY, else you will be cited as boarding the waterbus without a ticket and given a stiff fine.

TIP> You must validate your ticket at the Vaporetto stop or at the machine on the entrance to the Vaporetto. Insert it and just wait for the green light and the sound.
If you do not validate and the conductor inspects the ticket and finds you are out of time (75 minutes allowed or you do not validate on boarding) you will be fined on the spot.

TIP> If you will be in Venice 1, 2, 3 or more days and find it difficult walking, you might want to take a look at the multi-day passes.

You Need to Know Before You Go

You can also obtain an app and place your pass on your smartphone. It is best to check this out on the ACTV website.

TIP> The best day tour on your first day (if you have one day) in Venice is the Vaporetto Number Two "Cruise" down the Grand Canal. Follow the directions below and have your camera ready.
These directions are given as you come down the steps of the Santa Lucia rail station. Note you can board the #2 Vaporetto anywhere since it goes in a circle. If you board at St. Marks you will head first to the rail station. Just stay on the waterbus. It is best to consult a detailed map of Venice. Here are the details with a starting point of the Santa Lucia Stazione (rail station). It is best to start here about 10AM. You can of course pickup the #2 waterbus anywhere on the Grand Canal.

If you are coming out of the Santa Lucia Stazione you will see the #2 Vaporetto stop directly in front of you as you walk down all those steps to the canal. Note, watch out for the pigeons. Purchase a local ticket for 7.50 Euros from the black and yellow ACTV booth or use the machine. Both will take your credit card. All you need to say is "two" or "three" tickets. Each ticket is good for 75 minutes of travel. Make sure you validate.

Exit the Vaporetto at either of the Rialto stops. One stops at the far side of the Rialto Bridge and the other stops right near the market (Rialto Mercato) so you do not have to cross the bridge. If you are coming from the rail station, best is to exit the waterbus at the Rialto Mercato stop. Exit the Vaporetto and visit the market for about an hour or two.

TIP> Don't worry about missing that souvenir or whatever. You will see more of the same as you make your way over to St. Mark's Piazza. However, you will find very little fruit and other perishables en route, so best is to scoop up those items now.

ITALY Over 300 Critical Tips

TIP> You will find public restrooms at the market area. Remember to bring a one Euro coin for the matron who takes care of the facility.

TIP> Best also to bring your own toilet paper. Many of the public restrooms have toilet paper which feels like "crepe paper".

You should continue your walk by going over the Rialto Bridge.

TIP> The Rialto Bridge is a great place to take photos. It is also an excellent pickpocket location. Mind your items and only have a tourist couple take a photo of you with your smartphone or camera.
Also, avoid walking in the center of the bridge. Best is to hang on to one of the railings. Suggest you keep to your right all the time when crossing the bridges.

After going over the bridge with the market at your back you want to take a right at the base of the bridge and follow the traffic to the left of that church (Bartolomeo di Rialto).

Now follow those signs at the corner of the buildings and make your way to San Marco's square. It will take about 15 minutes.

On a one day visit you probably will only have time to visit one or two attractions in San Marco Piazza. The two major attractions which will not require a wait are Saint Mark's Basilica and the Doge's Palace. The Doges were the "kings" of the fiefdom known as Venice.

You can also go up to the top of the Campanile. It's that big bell tower in San Marco Piazza. It fell down in 1902 and was re-build about 10 years later. There is a great picture in black and white of a pile of bricks where the tower stood. It is available at several shops in the area. An elevator will whisk you to the top of the tower. The fee is 8 Euros and there is usually a wait.

You Need to Know Before You Go

About 12-1PM it's time for lunch.

TIP> If you want to spend $100 for lunch (two people) you can certainly have it at a café overlooking the Grand Canal. Check out the cafes on the Riva degli Schiavoni starting around the Hotel Danieli. If you really want an excellent lunch at a reasonable price visit the Taverna dei Dogi.
Finding the Taverna dei Dogi is quite easy. After you leave San Marco Piazza head to the water and take a left on Riva degli Schiavoni. Right after crossing the first bridge (Ponte della Paglia) take a left on Calle degli Albanesi. About one football field up (100 meters) you will find Taverna dei Dogi.

TIP> After lunch (or better before lunch) take a gondola ride for 40 minutes. They are parked at the gondola parking area directly in front of the Hotel Danieli. Assuming you are a couple (or at least two people in your group) the best is to see if you can get 4 other people to join you. In this way you can split the rate six ways. It should come out to about 25 Euros a person.
Also remember, the gondoliers (if that's what you call them) do not sing "oh solo meo". They do that only in Southern Italy. If you want a singer for a solo sunset gondola ride, check the internet and pre-arrange it.

Also, don't worry about hitting some big waves in the Grand Canal. The gondolas do not navigate the Grand Canal and take the first small canal to the left or the right of the Hotel Danieli.

TIP> After you are finished for the day (and probably "pooped") you need not walk back to your hotel. Just buy another ticket on the #2 Vaporetto or any Vaporetto bound for Santa Lucia Stazione (the Ferrovia). Don't worry if it's not going the correct way. You will still go up the Grand Canal or

one of those freight feeder canals. Depending on the schedule the waterbus may go the same way you came down to the Rialto area. Don't worry you won't get lost.

If you are not going to the rail station, do make sure you get off at the closest Vaporetto stop to your hotel.

TIP> Reserve your second or third days in Venice for the Peggy Guggenheim Museum or the Lido.

TIP> If it's a hot beach day consider taking your towels and your bathing suit in a day bag and head out for the Lido.

The Lido is a barrier island protecting the Lagoon. You can swim on the Adriatic side. The other side is part of the lagoon and is not really that clean to swim in, in fact, it's polluted.

If you are taking a Vaporetto, usually you need to change boats at one of the San Marco stops. It is best to consult one of the people at the black and yellow Vaporetto ticket booths, your hotel desk clerk or concierge can advise.

And, if it's not a beach day, the Lido is a great place for lunch, a stroll or a gelato.

TIP> If you have an extra day in Venice you may want to consider visiting the lagoon island of Murano which is best known for its glass blowing factories. The Vaporetto number 3 or 4.1 (slower) will take you there. Once again consult the ACTV booth. There is also a special boat which will get you there at no charge and drop you off at one of the glass blowing factories in hopes you will purchase a souvenir. It is best to consult with your front desk clerk.

# # #

CHAPTER 10

SECURITY

There are very few violent crimes committed in Italy each year. Few people have guns. In the last year, in all of Italy there were only 300 murders. In 2017, in the United States almost 40,000 people were murdered, quite a difference.

If you watch TV at night in Italy (RAI network) you will usually see game shows, soccer, or dance/music entertainment programs which are very much like "Sabado Gigante" which appears on Univision every week in the USA. You won't see TV programs which feature any type of violence except perhaps a re-run of an American western featuring John Wayne. Violent crime is pretty much non-existent in Italy. However, Italy makes up for this in what is known as petty crime.

Petty crime is basically "pick-pocketing" and other devious means to make you part with your wallet, passport, jewelry, or your laptop or something else of value.

I shouldn't single out Italy. It is just a common "nuisance" in most European countries and in fact all over the world but pretty much non-existent in America except on New Year's Eve in Times Square.

Read the following tips and be "Street Savvy".

ITALY Over 300 Critical Tips

---------- GENERAL RULES ----------

TIP> Try not to stand out as a tourist. The more you look like a local, the better it will be.
For men, leave that sport jacket home and forget those expensive pair of trousers and that elegant looking shirt. Instead wear a pair of blue jeans or khaki pants, better if they are khaki cargo pants. For women, best to wear Capri's and avoid fancy looking dresses or even sun dresses. For shoes, wear comfortable sneakers or walking shoes. And if you are there on your honeymoon don't dress for it. It is far better to dress down, else you will appear as a target for pickpockets and scammers. In other words DON'T FLASH.

TIP> Don't dress like an American or even an Italian who dresses as an American.
First, leave those ball caps and T-shirts that are truly American, home. If it says "HARVARD" or the ball cap says "PATRIOTS" leave it home. And, don't, repeat don't wear that sweatshirt which says ITALY or UNIVERSITY OF FIRENZE on it. Just pack it up and take it home.

Okay, you can certainly take one of those souvenir sweatshirts with you to dinner. However, I just wouldn't wear it on the Metro in Rome or in the city.

If you are outside of the major cities or in the Tuscan countryside strolling in the vineyards in the chilly morning, yes it's fine to wear that ITALY sweatshirt.

TIP> Never bring anything on a trip which you can't afford to part with, including your tablet or laptop.
I once took a trip to Sardinia (the island off the west coast of Italy) for a week. On arrival in Sardinia, I unpacked my bag only to find my gorgeous yellow and blue Nautica windbreaker gone. In fact, I even packed it with the sales tags still affixed. I

120

You Need to Know Before You Go

asked myself how could this happen? Simple, somewhere along the way, perhaps even when they inspected my bags in Rome to transfer to another flight, someone "pinched" my jacket. It happens all the time. What did I learn? Simple, it was one of my favorite jackets and I didn't even get a chance to wear it. I just should have brought one of my older jackets and if it was "pinched", no big deal.

To this day I do not bring my tablet or my laptop with me, only a smartphone. If I need to use a computer to send an elaborate email or a document, I find that most hotels either have a business center machine or will allow you to use one of their computers. If all else fails, I hunt down an internet café and invest 3-5 Euros to use their machine for an hour. No stress.

TIP> Ladies leave your good jewelry, and men leave that Rolex home!
I have heard too many stories and have read too many reviews, where a couple goes to breakfast in the hotel, the women leaves that beautiful "cocktail" ring on the night table only to come back and find it missing.

It is best to leave your fine jewelry home and take no jewelry at all. If you must wear a watch, take an inexpensive watch that you can afford to part with.

TIP> Remember to take your wallet and your smartphone with you to breakfast. Don't assume that everyone in the hotel is honest. Most of the time they are, and minor crimes are usually not committed by the hotel staff but by others.

TIP> Don't be alarmed that on check-in at your hotel you must surrender your passport. The desk person will give it back to you once they make a copy. You should remember to request it back the next day or before you depart.

ITALY Over 300 Critical Tips

TIP> Many older European hotels require you to drop off your room key at the front desk when leaving the hotel. Do not leave it on top of the counter so anyone can pick it up and use it. Give it to the front desk person or place it on the other side of the counter and not on top.

--------- AVOIDING PICKPOCKETS ---------

TIP> first realize that most pickpockets are looking for your money, then your passport and then your credit cards. All of them have some value. So for the money, you need a money belt or pouch.
I recommend the money belt available from Amazon B015HXS2QS. It's about $10. You can easily fold up six 100 Euro notes or six 50 Euro notes and zip them into the belt.

You can also use an under garment money pouch. However, if you are wearing one, make sure you use one of those large safety pins so as to pin it to your underwear. Take a look at Amazon B01G1ORT5M. This money pouch also adds RFID protection. Only problem with this money pouch is that when you go to the bathroom (and yes for women and men) it becomes somewhat of a hassle to unpin it and then pin it back.

TIP> Men, should carry a sacrificial wallet in your back pocket. Never carry your real wallet in your back pocket where it can be easily picked.
I carry two wallets with me. One is my regular wallet which I keep my hand on all the time in my front pocket and the other is my SACRIFICIAL WALLET which I keep in my back pocket. However, most of the time I wear those "cargo" pants so I don't have to keep my hand in my pocket. See my TIP below on what type of cargo pants and pockets.

You Need to Know Before You Go

Many years ago I asked my very wise father why he carried two wallets. He lived in New York City. He said, "Bob, you see this wallet I carry it in my back pocket. If they want to mug me or pick my pocket they get the sacrificial wallet". I asked him, what's in the sacrificial wallet? He said "all they will find is five dollars and some garbage receipts and some crappy discount cards you get in the mail that look like credit cards. So, if they pick my pocket, they will run down the street and think they scored a hit until they look at what they got...nada".

TIP> For men, if you can, wear those cargo pants and make it really difficult for a pocketpicker to remove anything without a struggle. Don't put anything of value in the type of pocket you need to zip up, you need to use those cargo pockets which have buttons not zippers.
This is an easy one. However, it just makes it more difficult to get anything out of those pockets once you put buttons on them. Pickpockets want to "hit" the victim and run, they won't hassle with buttons. What you can also do is take those pants to a tailor and just tell him/her to add two buttons to each of those zipper pockets. It will cost you a big $5-10 per pair of pants. Money well spent.

TIP> If possible wear a jacket with inside pockets with zippers. This is for the gents and the ladies.
This affords the best protection for your wallet and passport. You can also use one of those travel vests. However, make sure it has inside pockets.

TIP> In most European countries men have handbags just like the ladies. You will find it an excellent means to carry your wallet, keys, smartphone, maps, etc. However, you must have one with a strap which will go over and across your shoulder. Ensure the flap is turned inward toward your body, so it can't be easily opened.

123

ITALY Over 300 Critical Tips

TIP> Now for the ladies: Just like the men's bags you need to have a large handbag with a strap which you carry over and across your shoulder. Do not take your regular handbag as it can easily be torn from you i.e. "snatched".

TIP> Ladies, you must remember to put your wallet back in your bag. Don't just drop it in without re-zippering the bag.

A guest on one of my tours was purchasing a bottle of water at the McDonalds at one of the rail stations. As she put her wallet in the bag the pickpocket's "buddy" distracted her and in an eye-blink the pickpocket took the whole wallet out of her handbag. She only noticed she was missing her wallet when she went to purchase a soft drink on the train several hours later.

What she should have done before she walked up to the counter is removed a five Euro note from her wallet, placed the wallet back in her handbag and zippered it back up. The pickpockets know that you will open your wallet at the counter and that's the crux here. So don't open your wallet at the counter. It's likewise for the guys. Have your money ready when you present yourself at the counter to give the person your order. And PS, don't put the change in your wallet. Just stuff it in your pocket, or hold it in your hand until you are free of the counter.

TIP> This tip is for single young women and guys who like to wear backpacks.

You are at a major tourist attraction or using the subway and you are at a standstill. The person behind you just zips open the small compartment on the top of your backpack and presto, you passport is gone. Advice here is, don't put anything but tissues or napkins in these compartments. All your valuables should be in the main compartment of your backpack where the zipper is inaccessible unless you remove the entire backpack from your body.

You Need to Know Before You Go

TIP> If you are the type of person who likes to wear one of those fanny packs, DON'T wear it on your hip or your fanny (your butt). Instead you should wear it in front of you.

TIP> Most pickpockets use the distraction technique. They operate in teams or simple pairs. One of them distracts you while the other lifts your wallet, or whatever. All you need to remember here is to keep your guard up and do not get distracted. Here are some of the ploys:

There is a women beggar on the sidewalk or better what seems to be a small homeless child begging for some spare change. You feel so sorry for them. As you reach for your wallet or your pocket of change two others approach and start having an argument. As you turn around to see what's happening the other person grabs your wallet and off they go. Oh, and yes that poor boy was part of the setup!

You are walking down the street and the person next to you drops a handful of coins on the ground. As you offer to help him pickup the coins, you bend over (the guys) and bingo that wallet in your back pocket is picked by the other in the team. Hopefully, he took your sacrificial wallet and will be happy with the five Euro note, or better a one dollar bill and some expired gift cards to Dunkin Donuts, Home Depot and that red and white ad card from AARP.

Another variation of the above is the "jewelry drop". A woman is walking down the street and all of a sudden her necklace (it's the same type they use in New Orleans at the Mardi Gras parade) breaks apart and those cheap plastic beads spill all over the pavement. You reach down to help her and bingo your pocket book is grabbed by the other "team member".

I have also seen another type of jewelry drop. It actually was in Paris on a side street to the Champs Elysees. A man dropped

125

what appeared to be his wedding ring. As people try to help him by bending over and trying to find the ring, his partner makes a quick decision and hits one of the people bending over and removes their wallet from their back pocket. Once again hopefully it was a sacrificial wallet.

TIP> Never ask a single person to take your picture. This is a bad idea even if it's a single women that looks nice and sweet... it's a setup. Many times, they will even use young Asian ladies who look Vietnamese or Cambodian. You think they are tourists. Nope, they are part of the team! She may take your picture then get bumped by her "partner" who will run off with your new Iphone. Of course, she will say I am so sorry!

If you need someone to take your picture best approach is to spot another tourist COUPLE, a policemen or a shopkeeper who will take your picture. None of these people will run away with your smartphone.

TIP> Avoid "snatch and run" ploys. When walking on the sidewalk do not walk close to the curb, instead walk on the side away from the curb. Ladies should hold their bag over their shoulder, such that the bag is away from the curb. If you walk close to the curb you run the risk of a person on a motor scooter grabbing your bag and taking off at lightning speed.

TIP> Be extra cautious and vigilant in highly touristed areas. The Trevi Fountain in Rome is one such spot. Just take a look around you and you will see lots of police. And remember to keep those coins in your pocket and don't take out your wallet with that change purse. Also watch for people who

You Need to Know Before You Go

may bump you or get into your space.   If these "characters" invade your space, just move away.

When in these areas I do not remove my wallet from my cargo pants (the ones with the buttons on the pockets, not zippers) or better I keep my hand in my pocket on my wallet. In my hand I carry a 10 Euro note, so I do not have to take my wallet out to purchase a gelato! Hint here is..... you don't want to take out your wallet to remove Euros.

TIP> If you are taking the Rome subway system (the Metro) be extra cautious and avoid being the last one into the subway car. Pickpockets often can push you in and as they do this, you will part with your wallet or handbag as they run out of the station when your train pulls away. In other words, you will be on the moving train and they will be on the platform waving at you!

TIP> If you need to take out a tour book or a map and someone approaches you to help you, just say "no thanks" and "we are all set".

TIP> If you need to take out a tour book or a map don't do it in "open space". I usually, back up against a building where there is no one that can come from behind.

TIP> At a hotel if someone approaches you to help with your rollie or your carry-on and is not the official bellmen, just say no thank you.

TIP> If you are sitting down on a bench and someone sits next to you, simply get up and move.

TIP> In colder months, where you must place your jacket on a chair in a restaurant or café, try not to put it on top of someone else's or better make sure no one puts their jackets or coats on top of your yours!

TIP> Make photo copies of all your credit cards and keep them in a separate place. You can also keep them in your smartphone (assuming they haven't taken your smartphone).

TIP> Make copies of your passports and keep them in your bags back at the hotel. If you need to get replacements, all you need do is visit the American (or Canadian) embassy (in Rome) or consulate in other cities and usually within 24 hours you can obtain replacements.

TIP> In addition to pickpockets, be on the lookout for scammers. Here is how to avoid them.

There are persons roaming around the Coliseum and St. Peter's area who pretend to be licensed tour guides. In fact, they will be wearing badges which even look official. You see a big line waiting for tickets. The scammer approaches you and your girlfriend and says "Ladies I can take you on a 40 minute tour of St. Peter's for only 40 Euros and I can also whiz you through the security line with my official badge". After you accept his offer and pay him the 40 Euros, he will disappear into the security line and you will never see him again". Same goes in the Coliseum area. It is best to pay any of these tour guides only after the tour.

There are lots of other scams which are quite complex. Suffice it to be that if the offer is too good to be true, it's not true. So, just keep on walking.

You Need to Know Before You Go

--- OBTAINING CASH FROM ATM'S ---

TIP> Definitely avoid using the ATM after dark. Always visit an ATM in the daylight.

TIP> When visiting an ATM make sure you use the buddy system. Never visit the ATM alone.

TIP> If possible visit an ATM which is in a bank vestibule or better located in the bank. This provides maximum security.

You should avoid ATM's (BANCOMATS) which have no protection at all. In other words they are located on the street and anyone can stick their finger in your back and say "hand it over or else". They may also steal your wallet and your PIN.

TIP> Have your "buddy" (spouse, partner or other) on the lookout for anyone that looks suspicious or wants to invade your space.

Many times, potential pickpockets will have a cup of coffee or a gelato in a cone. While you are counting your money they will spill their coffee or dump their gelato on you, pretending it is an accident, then grab your money and run.

It is best to count your money and then put it in your pocket and not in your wallet. Place the money in your wallet or money belt when you return to your hotel room. The less time you spend at the ATM, the better it will be.

TIP> If you have time available, you should report any theft to the local police department and obtain a report of your filing, even if it's in Italian. For insurance purposes, make sure you tell the police exactly what was taken.

You probably will not get that cocktail ring back, but your insurance company may provide a replacement if you have it listed on your jewelry schedule of your homeowner's policy (or

HO6 policy if you have a rented apartment or home). If you cannot produce a police report you are out of luck and usually no replacement will be granted unless you have one of those "mysterious loss" clauses.

In summary, Italy is quite safe but, there are always those that will attempt petty crime. The best defense is to be vigilant all the time. Do not get distracted or enter into a potential "setup". Keep your bags zipped and heed the points I raised above. You may want to read them again on arrival in Italy.

CHAPTER 11

MONEY AND CREDIT CARDS

---------- MONEY ---------

Italy, as most of you know is on the European currency known as the Euro.

With the exception of taxi drivers who will usually accept your good old American dollars (with a stiff exchange rate) most other places will not. Ask yourself, if you were Italian and came over here with only Euros and wanted to pay your dinner bill in Euros, would they accept it. Probably not. Most places wouldn't even know what the Euro currency looks like.

So here is what you need to do:

TIP> If you are flying into Rome and taking the Leonardo Express into Rome's Termini station, you won't need any Euros as you can use your credit card to purchase your ticket. From the Milan airport (MXP) You can also use your credit card to purchase a ticket for the train to downtown Milan.

TIP> If you know someone who recently came back from a visit to pretty much anywhere in Europe ask them if you can purchase some Euros off them. Best to use the exchange rate in XE.COM.

TIP> After arriving at Rome airport you can purchase your Euros at an ATM machine. Best is to

locate a **BANCOMAT** machine. Avoid machines which do not say **BANCOMAT**. Bancomat is an association of banks which all "interline" with their machines. It's like the **INTERBANK CIRRUS** network in the USA and worldwide.

TIP> If you are taking the train into Rome, or renting a car, hold off buying Euros till you reach your destination as all the toll booths on the Autostradas (major toll roads) accept all credit cards. Also the cafes, gas stations, etc., on the Autostradas accept all credit cards.

TIP> At the airport, you should avoid the currency exchange booth's or the ATM's which do not have a bank name. They define the word "ripoff". They are basically the same as a cash machine you will find at a restaurant in the USA which does not take any credit cards. If you need cash they will point you to a bank card machine usually in the lobby where you can get some cash using your bank ATM card. They will add a fee on in addition to your regular bank fee if you have one.

Now here is how exchange rates vary:

I use these rates as a comparison but I think you get the point.

Say the XE exchange rate is $1.12 to buy one Euro. This is the rate the banks exchange at.

Now if you buy your Euros at your local bank (back in the USA) you will pay $1.30 for each Euro. You should avoid this option. Sometimes, there are even additional fees. It's pricey.

You Need to Know Before You Go

If you buy your Euros from the currency exchange booth (the cambio) at the airport or at the rail station you will pay $1.35 to buy one Euro. Yup, no commission, ha, ha, but a stiff rate.

If you use a BANCOMAT machine anywhere in Italy or a Bank ATM i.e. say Banca Monte dei Paschi di Siena (oldest bank in the world) you will pay $1.18 for each Euro.

If you swipe your bank card (a debit card) at any Trenitalia or any restaurant's credit card machine (assuming you select "pay in Euros") you will pay about the XE exchange rate say $1.12.

TIP> Do not purchase traveler's checks at AAA or your local bank. They are a thing of the past. In fact, many place's (including 4 and 5 star hotels) will charge you 5% or even 8% to take your traveler's checks, especially if they are in Dollars and not Euros.

TIP> There are BANCOMAT ATM machines (often called Cash Points) on practically every street corner in major tourist areas. All you need do is ask your hotel desk clerk or concierge where the nearest BANCOMAT machine is located and he will give you directions. I include how to use the BANCOMAT's in the Security Chapter.

TIP> It does not pay to take only 100 Euros out of the ATM at a time. If you add the fees you will find that you will be charged about 12-15%. However, you will be charged the same fees if you take out the maximum allowed per day. It varies by machine, the host bank and your bank. I always suggest 300 or 250 Euros on each withdrawal. When you get back to your hotel put 100 Euros in your wallet and stash

the rest in your money belt. Or better, have your partner hold it for you.

---------- CREDIT CARDS ----------

TIP> When paying with a credit card (or even a debit card), if offered to pay in Dollars or Euros, you ALWAYS want to select PAY IN EUROS. Why? It's simple.   The financial institution which the merchant is dealing with will NOT give you the bank transfer rate i.e. the credit card exchange rate or even the FOREX rate. They will add on a few cents and give you THEIR rate. It's the same when you go to a five star hotel in the USA. At the front desk they usually have a sign posted listing THEIR exchange rates and not the bank's.

TIP> Many credit card companies charge a FOREIGN TRANSACTION FEE for each foreign credit card transaction. So, you may receive your credit card bill when you return home of perhaps $2500 in foreign transactions.   Your credit card company may add (usually 3%) or $75 as a fee for no other reason to your bill. So it's best to find a credit card which has NO FOREIGN TRANSACTION FEE's. PS- when you apply and hopefully open the account you will be able to earn a boat load of points. It is best to consult the "thepointsguy.com" on the internet.

TIP> It is best to advise your credit card company that you will be in Italy for a certain time frame. In this way they know that your card number has not been compromised.   Many credit card companies allow you to do this on-line. The same is true with ATM bank cards.

You Need to Know Before You Go

TIP> In Italy and most places in Europe, when you a pay a bill using your debit or credit card, they will bring a special machine to you such that your credit card never leaves your possession. In the USA they do not do this.   Be wary of merchants or restaurants who will take your card.   If they don't bring you the machine or ask that you go to the front desk or hostess station (where the machine is located) to pay your bill, pay it in cash. I discussed this under the MEALS-FOOD Chapter, but it also applies to all merchants, gas stations, and more.

I make it a habit of never giving that wait person my credit card.   There are always some unscrupulous people that will copy all the information off your card and presto in a few months you get a charge from Italy. Bad idea! Always keep an eye on you card and never let it out of your possession.

I cover more on credit cards and money in the chapter on SECURITY Chapter.

# # #

CHAPTER 12

OTHER TIPS

TIP> If you are buying produce of any kind in a super market or a fruit stand, you cannot touch the items. If you are at an open market or whatever, don't go feeling the tomatos or the plums with your fingers. This is strictly forbidden. However, if you are in a super marcado (supermarket), look to where you will see those plastic bags. Next to them will be disposal gloves. You are expected to use the gloves and not touch the produce directly.

TIP> If you are really tired of walking around all day in Rome and do not want to take the Metro back to your hotel , best is to take a taxi. However, in Rome and Florence and other towns i.e. Siena, Lucca, etc., you cannot "hail" a taxi down. That's right, taxi's unlike cities such as New York and Chicago do not "cruise" looking for a fare. So here is how you get a taxi to take you back to your hotel. There are three ways:

Go to any hotel and ask the front desk or concierge to call you a taxi for you. And do take care of him with a one Euro coin and a "grazie". If it is a large hotel you probably will luck out and find taxis directly at the entrance to the hotel.

If you are close to a standup bar, do go in and ask the barista to call a taxi for you and have a café while you wait. And finally....

If you are lucky you can spot a taxi stand. You can also ask a shop keeper, a policemen or someone who knows the area

You Need to Know Before You Go

"Dove si trova un parcheggio dei taxi" or just fake it in English with "Dough vey e taxi stand" and hopefully they will assist.

TIP> Remember that most taxis with the exception of small towns charge by time and mileage. If you are stuck in traffic in Rome, that meter will still be running. It may be best to walk that final mile or duck into a standup bar and have some nourishment before continuing on. Hopefully, the traffic jam will subside or the accident removed from you path.

TIP> You do not have to tip the taxi driver. If it's short money, just tell him/her to keep the change (cambio). Taxi drivers do not expect a tip. You pay what the meter says. If the meter says 10 Euros 50 cents just give the driver 11 Euros and exit the taxi with a "grazie".

TIP> Italy is laid back. Bring items with you that you can wear several times and bring no items which you will rarely require.
Leave the tennis rackets at home. Ladies, do not bring those high heel shoes. Wear comfortable shoes, either walking shoes or sneakers. If you must, you can bring an additional pair of lightweight shoes for that special dinner. Few places in the major cities have swimming pools. So no need to bring those flip flops, bathing suits, etc. However, if coming in the shoulder months and you are up against July and August where the temperature will be quite warm, do bring your bathing attire especially if you are going to any beach area.

If it's your honeymoon or that special anniversary, it's acceptable for men to bring a sport jacket and ladies to bring a light weight dress. And yes, consider even buying an Italian sport jacket while in Italy. It's a real nice souvenir instead of one of those silly "snow globes".

ITALY Over 300 Critical Tips

TIP> Many towns and cities have street markets once or twice a week, especially the smaller towns. They usually start about 8AM and go till 2PM, when everyone goes home to take a siesta. On arrival at your hotel it is best to ask about the street market. I usually check the internet so I can plan my day accordingly. For example, if I am over nighting in Arpino I plan on arriving around the noon hour if I want to visit the street market on Saturday. It may mean starting out at 8AM instead of 10AM from my prior point.

TIP All locations in Italy are less than 90 minutes away from a beach unless you are up in the Alps abutting Switzerland. Consider going to the beach at Via Reggio about an hour from Florence via car or rail. Or better stay in Montecatini Terme instead of Florence.

Here are some other beach areas:

Rome- Ostia, just past the airport and reachable by train

Venice- The Venice Lido and Venice di Jesolo

Sicily- Lots of beaches – Mondello near the Palermo Airport

Most of the beaches in Italy will rent you a sun umbrella and chairs for as little as 20 Euros for the day. Many beaches have good facilities and offer free changing rooms. Make sure you bring a plastic bag to stash your wet bathing attire.

TIP> There is no need to bring every over-the-counter remedy with you. You will find a pharmacy pretty much on every block. Just look for the green lighted cross protruding from the building. You won't need your CVS, Walgreens or Rite Aid discount card as most of the pharmacies are still mom and pop owned.

You Need to Know Before You Go

TIP> If you haven't learned by now, cellular calling while travelling abroad is quite expensive and secondly you don't get a lot of minutes or data. Best approach is to definitely use WIFI from your hotel room in the evening to call home. There are many apps such as WHATSAPP, FACETIME, MESSENGER, SKYPE, GOOGLE VOICE to name a few. This will allow you to make a call over the Internet using your smartphone or tablet. If the call is made to another cell phone using WIFI on the Internet there is no charge. However, if you need to go off the Internet to a land line or another cell number i.e. 818-555-1982 (at the far end) not on WIFI, you will pay a few cents a minute for what is known as the termination charge. On Google Voice you will have to open an account and put perhaps $20 on it as a draw down likewise for Skype, etc.

At one time Verizon, had a $30 (per month) plan which offered 90 minutes of calling and 250Mb of data. Now because of all the tourists using WIFI/Internet the price has gone up to $70 per month for a small allowance of calling and data.

Texting with Verizon while in Europe is still quite cheap. As of this writing you don't need a plan at all. You will be charged $.05 to receive a text and $.50 to send a text. But don't start calling without a plan from Italy. It will cost you about $2 per minute. Do enquire about their travel plan of $10 per day when you do use it, instead of paying that $2 per minute; best to contact your mobile carrier.

TIP> This is really critical. Many cell phone users return home and find in a few weeks a staggering bill from their mobile carrier. Sometimes it can be as much as $200-600 extra for that trip to Italy. Yikes, what happened? Simple. You must deny the use of using 3G, 4G and 5G services from the Roaming Carrier i.e. Vodafone, etc. If you are on a

very limited data plan, perhaps 250Mbs you will exhaust that with 2-4 evenings on Facebook or sending photos back home. Best is to avoid these high data transfer applications unless you are strictly on WIFI in your hotel room. And to repeat... DENY MOBIL DATA or MOBIL ROAMING.

It's quite easy to do. All you need to do is go into your settings on your smartphone and deny your phone the ability to use the cell carrier. I won't go into all the details since it varies by carrier and type of phone. However, it is best to just call your carrier and find out exactly how to DENY ROAMING. In this way you will not be charged any expensive roaming fees for calls or data. In summary best is to text and use WIFI only.

It is difficult to control inbound calls. It is best to look at the number calling you and determine if you should take the call. There is no charge if you do not answer the call. Since I don't sign up for any travel plans now and make all my calls over WIFI from my room, internet café or restaurant, I refuse to answer any call. Most people will text me and if I have to make a long call I duck into a standup bar or internet café and use their complimentary WIFI while having my double espresso.

You Need to Know Before You Go

SUMMARY AND CONCLUDING WORDS

I hope you enjoyed reading this book as much as I enjoyed writing it and sharing my TIPs. Hopefully, you will use these TIPs on your first and subsequent visits to Italy.

If you want to do something different on that next trip to Italy, do consider "Palace or Castle Hopping" with my book *ITALY Skip the Hotel and Stay at a Palace...for the Same Price Live Like Royalty*.

And as a final thought.....

It is believed Mark Twain (or someone else) stated the following:

"Twenty years from now you will be more disappointed by the things you didn't do than by the ones you did do. So throw off the bowlines, sail away from the safe harbor. Catch the trade winds in your sails. Explore. Dream. Discover."

Ciao for now.....

Bob Kaufman

Made in the USA
Monee, IL
07 March 2024

54632619R00085